INTERNATIONAL GRAPHIC DESIGN, ART & ILLUSTRATION

Editor: YUSAKU KAMEKURA

Publisher: RECRUIT CO., LTD.

Production: RECRUIT CREATIVE CENTER

Printing: TOPPAN PRINTING CO., LTD.

Distributors: NIPPON SHUPPAN HANBAI INC.
WILLIAM E. YAMAGUCHI ASSOCIATES INC.
RECRUIT EUROPE LTD.

編集長 ——————— 亀倉雄策

編集アシスタント ——————— 菊池雅美

アートディレクター ——————— 亀倉雄策

デザイナー ——————— 水上 寛

アシスタントデザイナー —— 加藤正巳
　　　　　　　　　　　　　廣田由紀子

プリンティングディレクター —— 小嶋茂子

英訳 ——————— ロバート・ミンツァー

発行 ——————— 1993年9月1日

定価 ——————— 3,200円 (本体3,107円)

発行所 ——————— 株式会社 リクルート
　　　　　　　　　〒104 東京都中央区銀座 8-4-17
　　　　　　　　　TEL.03-3575-7074 (編集室)

発行人 ——————— 位田尚隆

制作 ——————— リクルートクリエイティブセンター

印刷 ——————— 凸版印刷株式会社

用紙 ——————— 特漉NKダルアート 日本加工製紙株式会社

発売 ——————— 株式会社六耀社
　　　　　　　　　〒160 東京都新宿区新宿 2-19-12 静岡銀行ビル
　　　　　　　　　TEL.03-3354-4020 FAX.03-3352-3106

世界のグラフィックデザイン, アート & イラストレーション

クリエイション

編集——亀倉雄策

発行——株式会社リクルート
制作——リクルートクリエイティブセンター

印刷——凸版印刷株式会社
発売——株式会社六耀社

Editor ——————— Yusaku Kamekura

Editorial assistant ——— Masami Kikuchi

Art director ————— Yusaku Kamekura

Designer ————— Yutaka Mizukami

Assistant designers —— Masami Kato

Yukiko Hirota

Printing director ——— Shigeko Kojima

Translator ————— Robert A. Mintzer

CREATION No.18 1993

Publisher ————— Recruit Co., Ltd.
8-4-17 Ginza, Chuo-ku, Tokyo 104, Japan
TEL. 03-3575-7074 FAX. 03-3575-7077 (Editor's Office)

Production ————— Recruit Creative Center

Printing ————— Toppan Printing Co., Ltd.

Distributors ————— Nippon Shuppan Hanbai Inc.
4-3 Kandasurugadai, Chiyoda-ku, Tokyo 101, Japan
TEL. 03-3233-1111 FAX. 03-3233-1578

William E. Yamaguchi Associates Inc.
225 East 57th Street, New York, N.Y. 10022 USA
TEL. 212-753-1224 FAX. 212-753-1255

Recruit Europe Ltd.
2/3 Bedford Street, London, U.K., WC2E 9HD
TEL. 071-497-8800 FAX. 071-836-0999

© 1993 by Recruit Co., Ltd.

Printed in Japan

CONTENTS——目次

表紙：ソール・バス

Cover: SAUL BASS
表紙：ソール・バス

6

TRAVEL 旅

Yusaku Kamekura 亀倉雄策

As I sip my morning coffee, I am watching an art program on TV. It's about an artist who travels the world painting landscapes. For a few brief moments, the scene shifts to the Italian island of Sicily. It shows steeply terraced cities with ancient castles and narrow lanes, a scene of striking beauty in uniform tones of brownish gray. The moment I see it, my heart skips a beat. I turn to my wife: "Come to think of it, we've never been to Sicily, have we. It sure looks like it would be a great place to visit." A few minutes later, I'm out on our balcony sitting at a small white table, writing this essay in the cool, leafy shade of a large beech tree. A refreshing breeze stirs from time to time, causing pockets of sunlight to dance across the table.

More than the great metropolitan centers of Europe, personally I prefer the smaller country towns. I once spent about ten days traveling between Rome and Milan, taking in the seaside fishing villages, the quaint churches and the mountaintop burgs straight out of the Middle Ages. Shunning the main highways, I traveled exclusively by country road. That was a long forty years ago. Then just last spring I traveled from Milan to Florence, this time by highway. My expectations of viewing some lovely rustic country-side were thoroughly dashed. Continuing on from Florence to San Gimignano by country roads, however, I reveled in the bucolic charms characteristic of the Tuscany region: the gently rolling hills, the isolated old farmhouses, the flowering trees in their gardens. No matter where you look, every scene is pretty as a picture.

My various travels in Italy have covered nearly the entire country, yet somehow I seem to have missed Sicily. Apparently, Sicily is quite different architecturally from the Italian mainland. Pictures of its 16th and 17th-century churches, for example, reveal beautiful decorative sculpture of powerful impact. Of course, rather than pictures I'd prefer to see this artwork first-hand. If I have such an urge to go, you might wonder, then why don't I just drop everything and go? Well, it's not as simple as all that. In fact, it's nearly impossible. This is because, unlike an artist or a poet, a designer can't just take off suddenly on a journey at whim when social and business responsibilities are waiting. That's not to say that designers don't think about taking time off to travel at our leisure—indeed we do. Everyone longs to experience totally different cultures. It's a kind of spiritual longing. When that longing also has an element of romanticism about it, though, in most cases such yearnings go forever unfulfilled. At least, that seems to be the fate that awaits most people.

One of my all-time favorite books, which I first read many years ago, is John Steinbeck's *Travels With Charley*. It describes a journey which the author made around the United States between September and December in 1960. He and his traveling companion, Charley, an old French poodle, traveled in a truck whose bed was customized to serve as sleeping quarters. What made their trip unique was their avoidance of highways in favor of slower country roads. In Steinbeck's view, highways may get you to your destination faster, but they lack all human drama: they represent the insipidity of our modern culture. In one episode, for example, he

朝のコーヒーを飲みながらテレビの美術番組を見ている。ひとりの画家が風景を描きながら世界中を旅行する。そのなかで、ほんの2カットだがイタリアのシチリア島の風景が出た。17世紀の段々になった城の街と細い路地のたたずまいであった。その風景は渋い茶がかった灰色のトーンで統一されて美しかった。それを見た瞬間、私の胸がキューンと音をたてた。となりでテレビを見ていた妻に「そうだ、俺はシチリアには行ったことがなかったなあ。なんとか行ってみたいね」と言った。

やがて、その美術番組が終った。私はベランダに白い小さなテーブルを持ち出して、この原稿を書いている。ベランダすれすれに前と横にブナの大木が枝を広げて、涼しい陰をつくってくれる。ときおり木陰を抜ける爽やかな風。木漏れ日が白いテーブルにチラチラとゆれる。

私はヨーロッパの代表的な大都市よりも地方の小都市のたたずまいが好きだ。ミラノからローマまで10日間かけて、漁村や教会や中世のままの山の上の村などを廻った。ハイウェイは避けて田舎道だけを走った。もう40年も前の話である。昨年の早春、ミラノからハイウェイでフィレンツェまで行ったが、期待したような田園風景は少なくて落胆した。しかし、フィレンツェからサンジミニヤーノまでは田舎道を走ったので、トスカーナ地方特有の田園風景が美しく魅力にあふれていたのに満足した。ゆるい丘陵の畑、点在する古い農家、その農家の庭の木が白い花をつけていた。だから、どこを切り取っても見事な絵になってしまう。

私はイタリアのほとんどを廻ったつもりだったが、どういう訳かシチリア島だけは行っていない。シチリアはイタリア本土と違った様式を持った建造物が多いらしい。16、17世紀の教会の写真などを見ると、装飾彫刻の見事な様式美は強い造形となって迫ってくる。だから写真でなく実物を自分の目で見たいと思ってしまう。それは未知なものに対する興味であり、また憧れでもある。そして、憧れが夢のような想像をかきたてるのだ。かきたてるから、じゃあ旅に飛び出せるかというと現実は簡単じゃない。むしろ実現不可能に近い。それは、デザインという仕事は社会的な責任やビジネスがからんでいて、画家や詩人のように自由気ままに旅に出るということが出来ないからだ。そのくせ、いつかは時間をつくって、のんびりと旅をしたいと誰でも考える。自分の住んでいるところと違った文化を体験する。それは一種の精神の冒険なんだが、その冒険にはロマンがあると憧れながら、遂に希望もむなしく一生を終えるのが一般的な人たちの運命のような気がする。

私がずいぶん昔に読んだ好きな本に、ジョン・スタインベックが書いた『チャーリーとの旅』がある。スタインベックが1960年の9月から12月にかけて、自らトラックを運転してアメリカ全土を一周する旅行記である。トラックといっても、荷台を簡単に寝泊り出来るように特別に改造したものだ。そして、チャーリーという老プードル犬を相棒として、一緒に旅する。注目する点は、ほとんどハイウェイを利用しないで、すべて田舎道をトコトコ走ったことだ。ハイウェイは早く目的地に着くが、その道程には人間の生活の臭いがしない。現代文明の味気なさだけ

describes coming upon a young girl selling freshly picked fruit in a basket by the side of the road near a small farm. As Steinbeck continued his journey, however, he gradually grew distressed to discover that the America of the "good ole days" was rapidly disappearing. He was also saddened to see how television was eroding local dialects, causing the gradual spread of "standardized" English everywhere.

As he travels his country byways, Steinbeck delights in the unpretentious warmth he finds in the out-of-the-way towns and villages. One day he stops for the night beside a lake. You can easily picture him setting there before a roaring campfire, his aging companion by his side and a bourbon in his hand. Suddenly a man appears out of the nearby woods. He politely asks Steinbeck if he might join him by the fire. He says he is just drifting around with no particular destination in mind. Recognizing his loneliness, Steinbeck hands him a glass of bourbon. The man takes a swig, and then begins talking about his travels. Steinbeck listens intently, nodding his head every so often. Naturally, the man hasn't the slightest notion that this man who has so kindly shared his whiskey with him would soon become a Nobel Prize-winning author. This is what makes traveling so wonderful... and so poetic.

The mention of poetry reminds me of a little-known Japanese poet named Santoka, who lived slightly before Steinbeck and spent nearly his entire life traveling. Santoka was a master of haiku, the poetry form of only 17 syllables that demands great compression of one's words and thoughts, a complete trimming of all but the essentials. Santoka's life followed suit, for to pursue his poetic aspirations Santoka left his wife and children and became a wandering monk. Draped in his priestly robes he traveled continuously, living off offerings of rice and a few coins from people along his way. At night he would rest wherever he might: under the eaves of someone's home, in a village prayer hall, or in the shadows of a rocky cliff. Unlike Steinbeck, a man of great fame who traveled in anonymity, Santoka was utterly unknown from the start. He proceeded from one destination to the next, begging for alms to sustain him and writing his poems. His poetic talents were recognized during his life only by a handful of like-minded haiku exponents; the world at large was unmoved. In the end, he died far from home, nameless and alone.

What is the true purpose of travel? Travel is a personal adventure. For some it may be a lifelong journey sustained by begging for alms. For others it may be a sojourn carried out incognito to conceal one's fame. Either way, travel is an expression of each individual's lifestyle. It has been said that from birth till the moment of death, we are all on one continuing journey; then we start on a second journey anew.

I see a forest of young trees before me. Behind them is a lake, glistening. The cicadas, so raucous until just a moment ago, have suddenly grown eerily silent, no doubt because the sun has gone half-hidden behind the mountains. A chill comes over me. The lake will soon be blanketed in mist, for sure.

である、とスタインベックは考えたのだ。彼のトラックが小さな農村の入口にさしかかると、小さな女の子がもぎたての果物をざるに入れて道ばたで売っていたりする。しかし旅行を続けてみると、アメリカの古き良き時代が急速に遠ざかってゆくのに心が痛んだ。テレビの普及で言葉が標準語になり、次第に地方特有の方言が失われてゆくのも淋しい。

田舎道をゆっくり走らせ、小さな村で素朴な人情にひたりながら村々を通り過ぎ、落日に光る湖のほとりでキャンプする。焚火を前にバーボンの水割りを飲みながら、老犬と一緒にはじける火をみつめているスタインベックの後姿が目に浮かぶ。その時、林の灌木をかきわけて男がやって来る。ていねいに、焚火に当たってもいいかときく。車で目的もなく旅を続けているのだという。男は淋しかったのだ。スタインベックからバーボンの水割りを手渡されて、ひとくち飲んでから旅の話をぽつりぽつりと語りだす。町で起きたこと、村で起きたこと。時たまスタインベックは相槌を打つが、じっと男のしゃべるのを聞いている。男は目の前のバーボンの水割りを渡してくれた人が、ノーベル文学賞に輝く大文豪だとは露ほども知らないのだ。そこが旅の素晴らしいところだ。そして旅には詩があると思う。

詩で思い出したが、日本の詩人でスタインベックよりも少し前の時代の、山頭火という人が人生のほとんどを旅で暮した。山頭火は近年急に注目され出した詩人である。日本の詩というのは、一番短い俳句、少し長い短歌、そして西洋風に長い現代詩がある。山頭火は短い俳句をつくる人だ。俳句は言葉を切り詰め、切り詰め17文字で表現しなければならない。身を削るような詩作である。彼は詩作のために家を棄てる。妻子を棄てて僧侶となって漂泊の旅に出る。歩行禅という行乞の旅である。要するに僧衣をまとって、家々を托鉢して米や小銭をもらって旅を続ける。民家の軒下、村はずれの御堂、岩陰に身をひそめて寝た。スタインベックは高名なるがゆえに、逆に無名の男となって旅をしたが、山頭火は全く無名で、乞食のように身を落として詩作の旅を続けた。極限まで自分を追い詰めて、自然を凝視し、自然を摑み取った。彼の才能は、ほんの一握りの俳句仲間が評価しているだけで、決して世間一般からもてはやされたというものではなかった。だから彼は無名のまま、故郷を遠く離れた地で淋しく死んだ。

いったい旅とはどういう意味を持つものか。旅に詩があると憧れる。でもそれは旅のほんの一面でしかない。旅は体験的な冒険。といっても乞食までして旅で果てる人。高名を秘して、ひたすら普通人として旅をする人。旅はそれぞれの人生を表現しているように思う。人間は生まれた時から死ぬ瞬間まで旅を続ける。それから別の旅が始まる、とある宗教家が言った。

目の前に、低い木々が広がっている。その向こうに湖が光って見える。さっきまで波のように高く低く鳴いていた蟬の声が、うそのように静かになった。陽光が半分山の後ろに隠れたからだ。急に冷気を感ずる。きっと、もうすぐ湖面に霧が立ちこめるに違いない。

FRANCISZEK STAROWIEYSKI フランチシェク・スタロヴェイスキ

Jan Sawka ヤン・サフカ

In the great constellation of Polish poster stars of the last 35 years, Franciszek Starowieyski occupies a very special place. His talent is immense: he possesses great drawing skills and a truly masterful sense of space and color. From the beginning of his career he has followed his own path, ignoring passing trends and fancy styles.

Starowieyski's art seems firmly based in the past. The masters of Italian art, the Dutch painters and the German etchers of the 17th century all figure among his natural influences. Starowieyski never hides these connections; on the contrary, he often signs his works "1682" instead of "1982."

It is important to recognize that Starowieyski is not only a graphic artist: he is equally at home in the theater. His outstanding theater posters are often accompanied by strikingly innovative set designs, for both classical and modern plays. Some years ago he crossed yet another new border, developing his own "Theater of Drawing." In a large space created by canvassed frames, he draws his visions live, before a changing audience. The process takes several days at least, sometimes as long as a week.

The mostly theatrical posters featured in this issue present some of the most important strong points of his style. Starowieyski masterfully portrays traumatic sexual relationships between people, the dark mental deterioration of the heroes of dramas, cruelty and the passions of love and hate. His visual vocabulary is rich and metaphysical, surreal and magical all at the same time. His anatomical mastery of the human and animal body is splendid; yet the artist deforms the faces and torsos, adding a sense of drama and tragedy.

Many of Starowieyski's works are pure studies of human madness. Others show the piercing intelligence of the artist in commenting on the political events of his time and his country. Two such masterpieces may be singled out here. One is his poster for Franz Kafka's play about claustrophobic confinement to a small room. It is a dramatic study of the intellectual imprisonment which was present for so many centuries in Starowieyski's part of Europe. The second work is the poster for Mickiewicz's play addressing the long and tragic struggle of Poland for freedom. The march of fallen heroes and the struggle encompassing many generations are depicted with brilliance and simplicity.

Starowieyski's mastery of drawing is always striking. His deformation is amazingly well conducted. His colors, if any, are developed with a great sense of balance. And the text is so integrated with the picture, we have the feeling we are seeing a pure work of fine art, not a commissioned poster.

Despite his declarations of having no interest in politics and contemporary events, Starowieyski's art sends us a powerful message. His tormented mind cries out a personal protest against the growing paranoia of society. He tries to hide himself behind the cover of the Old Masters style and carefully restricts his territory to the theatrical stage. But within the territory of his choice we are all spectators of a great and magical personal theater named Franciszek Starowieyski.

この35年の間にポーランドポスター界が生んだそうそうたるスターたちの中で、フランチシェク・スタロヴェイスキは非常に特異な存在である。並外れたドローイングの技術と優れた空間や色彩のセンスを持ち、その才能には計り知れないものがある。彼は初めから、流行や凝ったスタイルを追うことなく、独自の道を歩んで来た。

スタロヴェイスキのアートは、しっかりと過去に根ざしているように見える。イタリア美術の巨匠たち、オランダの画家たち、17世紀ドイツの版画家たち。彼にはそうした人々の影響が自然に現われている。スタロヴェイスキはこのような関わりを決して隠すことなく、むしろ作品に「1982年」と記すかわりに「1682年」と書いたりする。

スタロヴェイスキは、単なるグラフィックアーティストではないと認めることが大事である。彼は演劇にも同じ位精通している。古典劇、現代劇を問わず素晴らしいポスターを作るほかに、併せて極めて革新的な舞台装置をデザインすることも多い。数年前彼は「ドローイングの劇場」を展開し、さらに新しい境地を開いた。入れ代わる観衆の前で、巨大なキャンバスに自分のビジョンを描いたのだ。それは少なくとも数日を要し、1週間かかったこともある。

今回は主として演劇ポスターが紹介されているが、そこには彼の作風の最も大きな特徴が見られる。人々の間のショッキングな性的関係、劇の主人公たちの暗い精神的な退廃、残酷さ、そして愛と憎しみの激情といったものが見事に描かれているのだ。その表現方法は豊かであり抽象的、シュールであり不思議である。人体や動物の解剖学的な描写は優れているが、劇的あるいは悲劇的な感じを出すために顔や胴体はデフォルメされている。

スタロヴェイスキの作品の多くは、人間の狂気をありのままに描いている。また当時自国で起こった政治的な事件を批判した作品もあり、そこに彼の鋭い知性を感じることができる。なかでも代表的な2つの作品をここに挙げよう。ひとつは小部屋に閉所恐怖症者を監禁するという話の、フランツ・カフカの演劇のポスターである。このポスターはスタロヴェイスキの住む東ヨーロッパでは何世紀もの間行なわれた、思想の「監禁」を表現した印象的な作品といえる。2つめはポーランド民主化への長く悲惨な闘いを描いたミキエヴィッチの演劇のポスター。倒れた英雄たちの行進と何世代にもわたる闘争が見事にそして率直に描かれている。

スタロヴェイスキのドローイングの技術にはいつも目をみはるものがある。デフォルメが驚くほど巧みに施され、色彩には優れたバランス感覚がある。そして文字は絵と調和し、商業的なポスターではなく、ファインアート作品を見ているかのような気にさせられる。

政治や今日の出来事には何の関心もないと明言するスタロヴェイスキだが、彼のアートは力強いメッセージを私たちに伝える。彼の痛めつけられた精神は、社会に増大するパラノイアに強く抵抗している。彼はその気持ちを過去の巨匠たちのような作風の裏に隠そうとし、用心深く仕事を演劇という範疇に限定している。しかしその中で私たちはみな、フランチシェク・スタロヴェイスキという名の、素晴らしい不思議な劇場の観客となるのである。

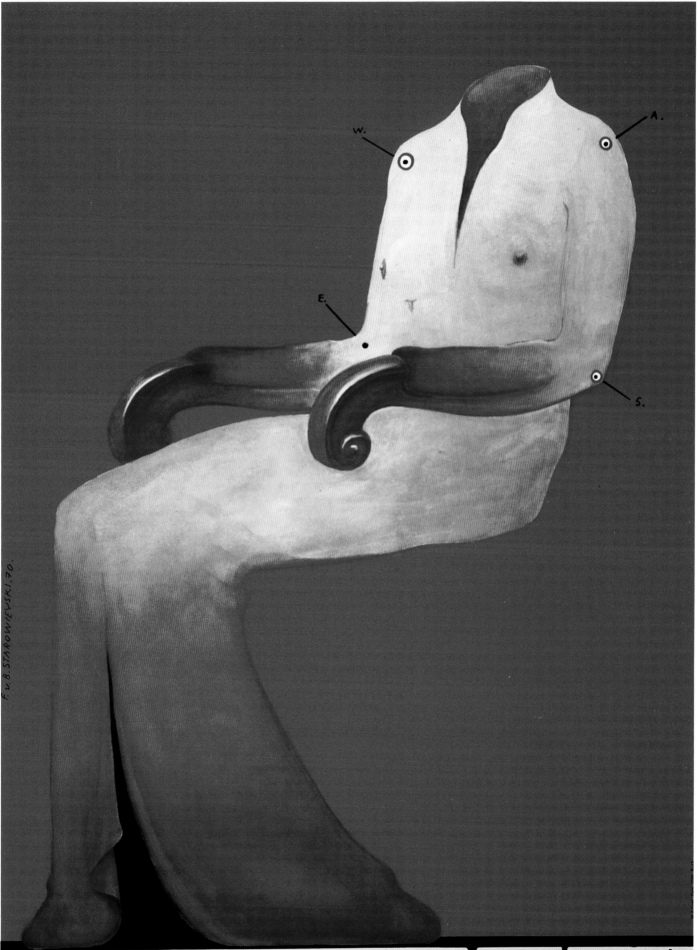

F. v. B. STAROWIEYSKI. 70.

1 Theater poster 演劇ポスター 1970

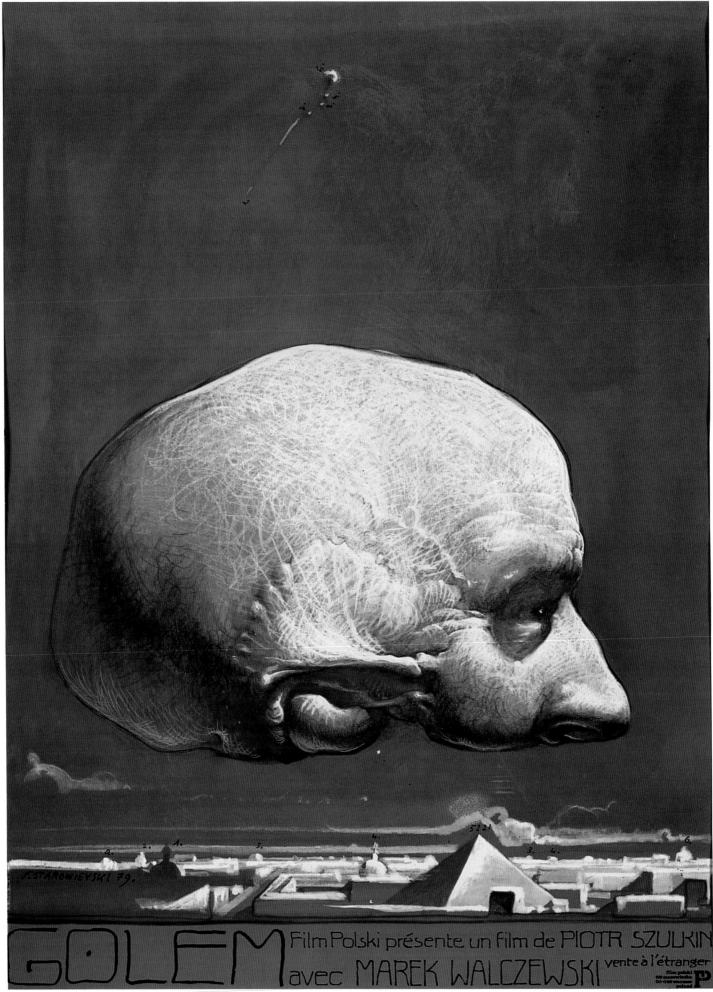

2　Film poster　映画ポスター　1979

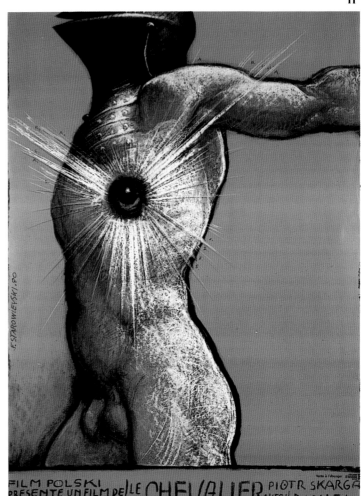

4 Film poster 映画ポスター 1980

3 Theater poster 演劇ポスター 1980

5 Theater poster 演劇ポスター 1979

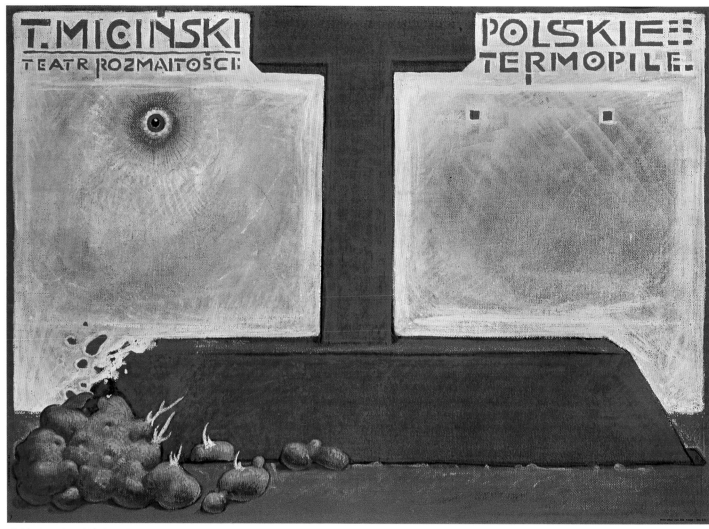

6　Theater poster　演劇ポスター　1982

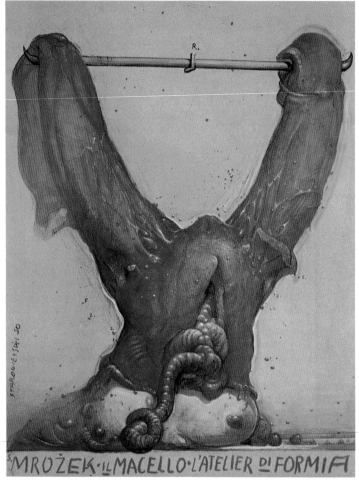

7　Theater poster　演劇ポスター　1980

9 Theater poster 演劇ポスター 1976

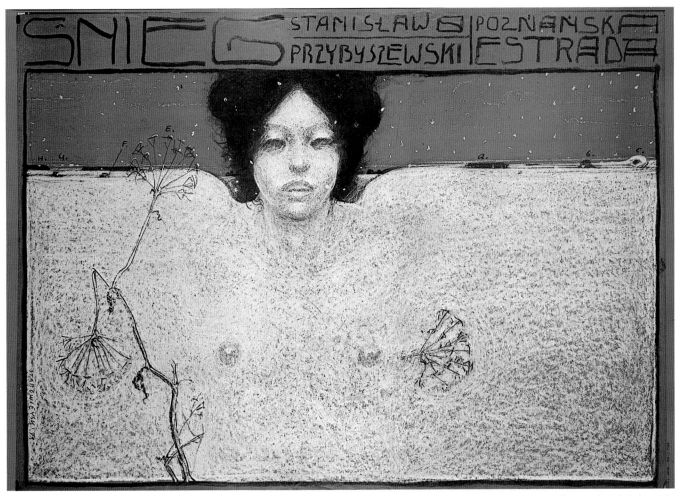

10 Theater poster 演劇ポスター 1979

11 Theater poster 演劇ポスター 1978

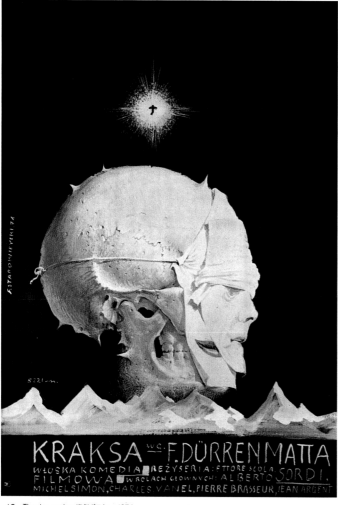

12 Theater poster 演劇ポスター 1974

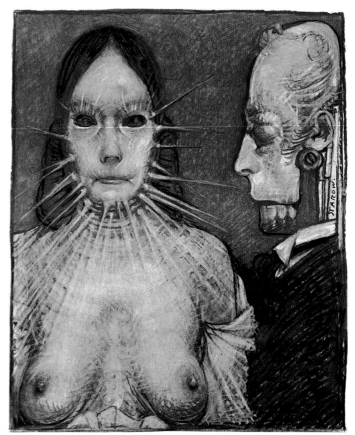

14 Theater poster 演劇ポスター 1974

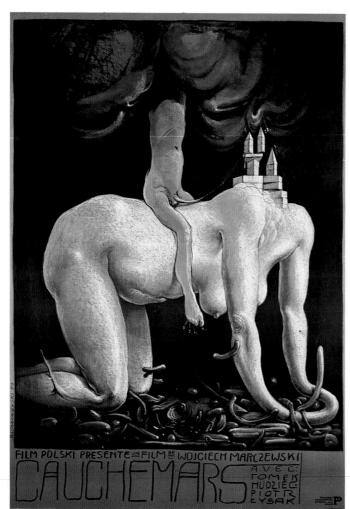

13 Theater poster 演劇ポスター 1979

15 Theater poster 演劇ポスター 1983

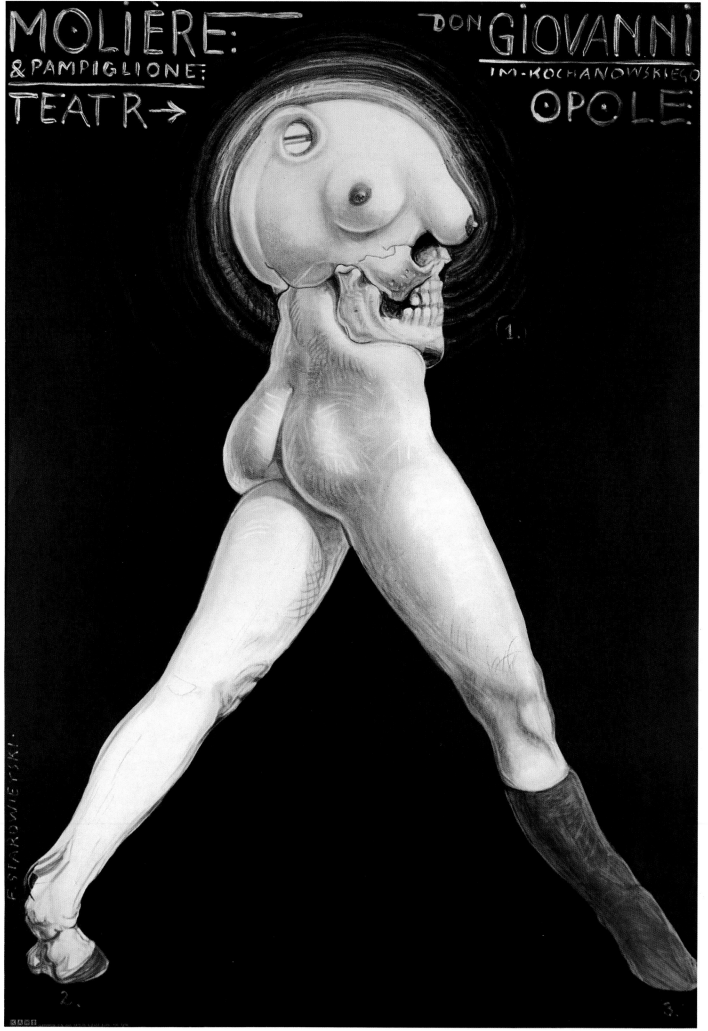

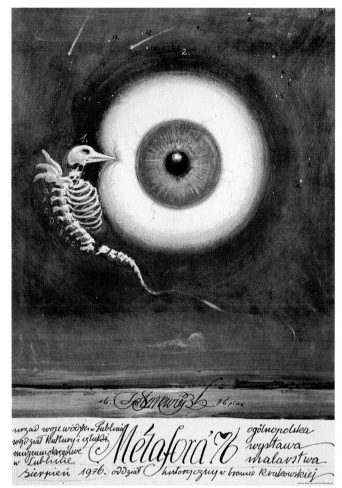

17 Exhibition poster 展覧会ポスター 1976

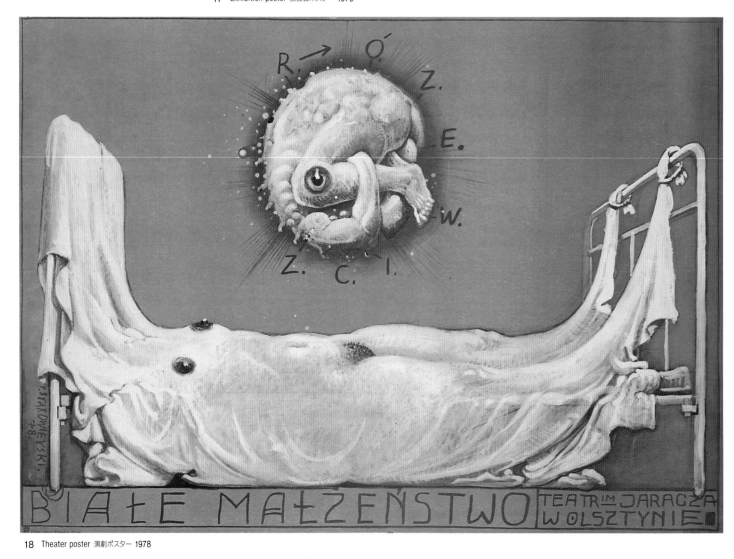

18 Theater poster 演劇ポスター 1978

21 Performimg arts poster パフォーマンスのポスター 1979

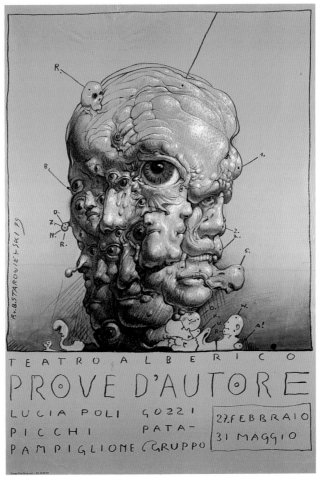

22 Theater poster 演劇ポスター 1979

MICKIEWICZ DZIADY

Sz.P. z. 118. n. 1500 E-5/228

23 Theater poster 演劇ポスター 1984

24 Theater poster 演劇ポスター 1976

25 Theater poster 演劇ポスター 1983

26　Theater poster　演劇ポスター　1975

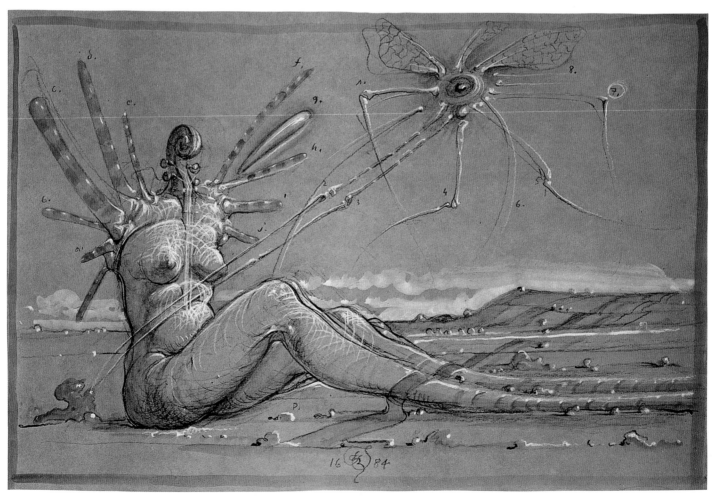

27　Poster for music festival　音楽祭のポスター　1984

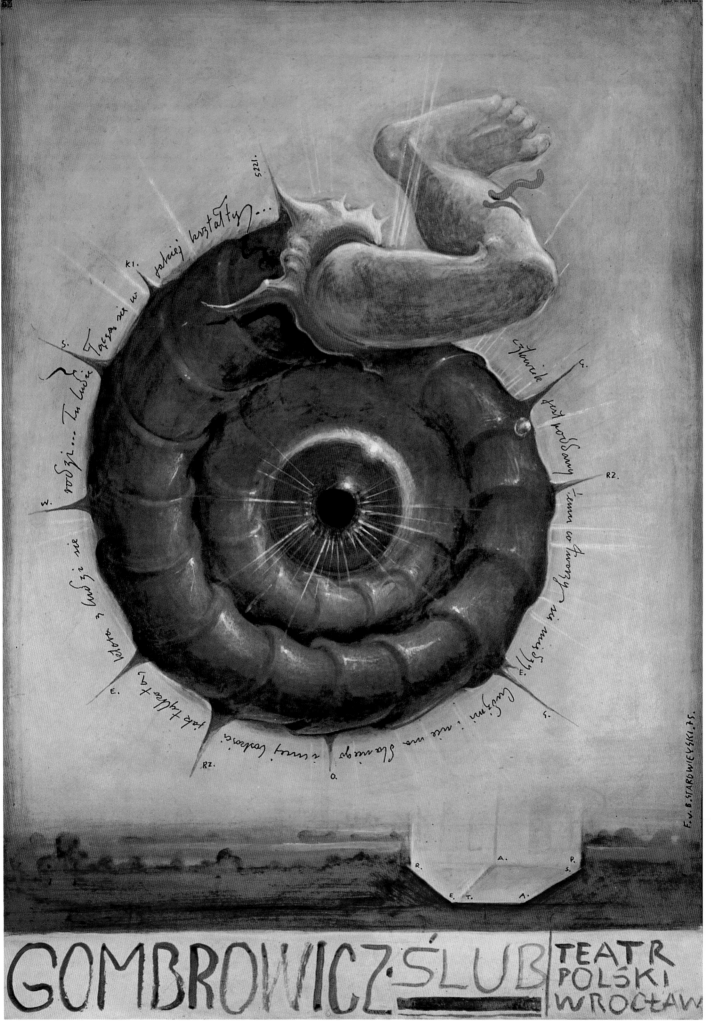

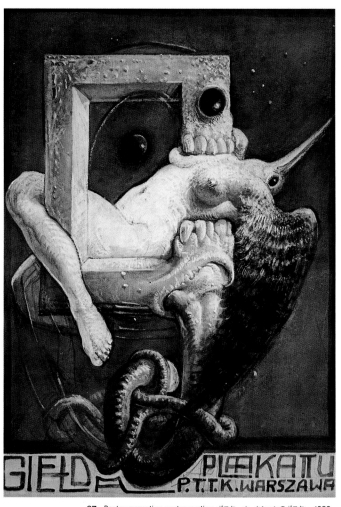

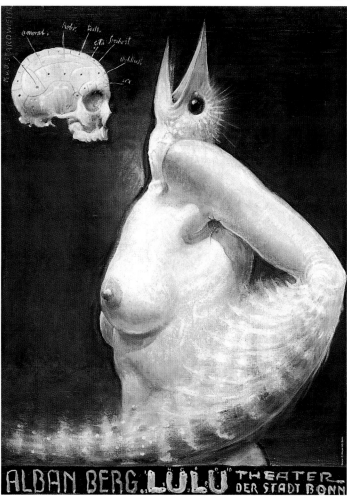

37　Poster promoting poster auction　ポスターオークションのポスター 1982

38　Theater poster　演劇ポスター 1979

FRANEK STAROWIEYSKI

39　Exhibition poster　展覧会ポスター 1978

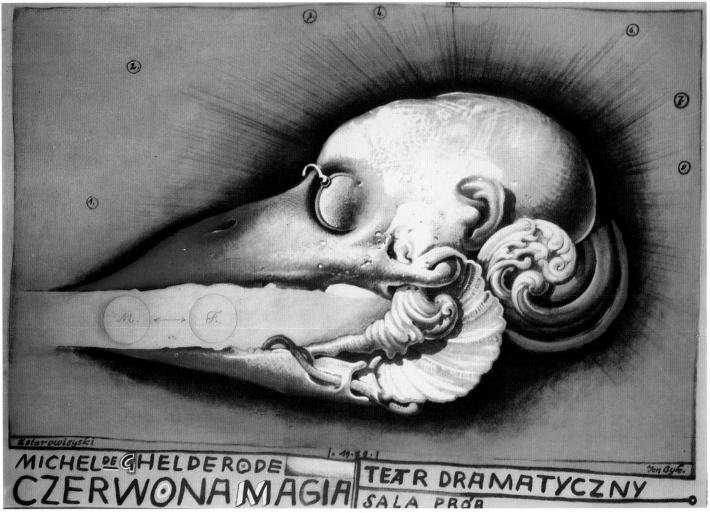

40 Theater poster 演劇ポスター 1971

41 Film poster 映画ポスター 1973

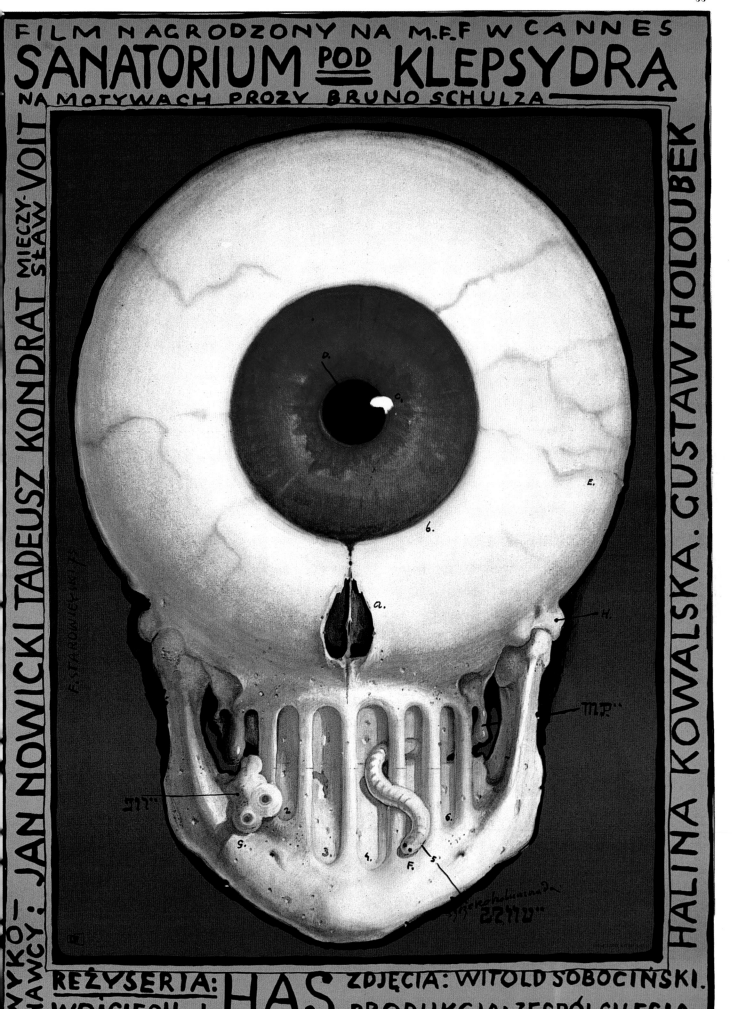

SAUL BASS ソール・バス

Henry Wolf ヘンリー・ウルフ

In the spring of 1956 I was standing in line in the ballroom of the Waldorf Astoria hotel waiting to go up to the podium to receive my first gold medal of the New York Art Directors Club. I was very nervous. I had worn uncomfortable shoes and taken them off under the table during lunch. When my name was called, I forgot to put them back on. In my socks, not daring to go back to the table, I stood behind a very friendly-looking, lovable sort of man with a brush of a moustache. He seemed so relaxed that I felt even worse. He nodded "Hello!" with this inimitable expression of his that infers that everything that is going on is a sort of joke. Three minutes later, when they announced his name to get a medal for one of his film titles—I believe it was *Man with the Golden Arm*—I knew that I had met Saul Bass. Ten years went by until our next meeting at the Aspen Design Conference. By then I knew much more about him and his work. (How could anyone in our business not know when there are so many reminders all around us?)

I had seen another dozen of his film titles, most of them a result of his stormy but wonderful collaboration with Otto Preminger. There was *Walk on the Wild Side* (my favorite) and *Exodus* and Hitchcock's *North by Northwest*. With Hitchcock too he directed that classic chilling shower sequence in *Psycho*. There was that marvelous short film *Why May Creates* which compresses civilization without losing either facts or that humor about the world which I was quick enough to detect during our first meeting. There was the car racing in *Grand Prix* and the battle in *Spartacus*—and so many others. His recent film *Quest*, in full collaboration with his wife Elaine, is an odyssey through a magical, surreal world in which, once again, life is compressed into an eight-day span. A child is set forth to reach the mythical door to light and liberation. Ray Bradbury's script and the wonderfully simple and yet complex effects (without the cliches of the expensive space films) convey a sense of mystery and danger in their bluish greyness, which is in sharp counterpoint to the last few minutes when the child who has become a man in a few days reaches freedom and long life.

By itself this sounds like the work of a lifetime. But you run into Bass's imagery everywhere you turn, anywhere in the world. We were recently in Israel together and, driving through the desert, we passed an Esso petrol station. I knew Bass had designed the prototype. I looked at him and he just nodded. It must be strange to run into yourself everywhere, at any airport where the United Airlines planes are lined up bearing Bass's "double U"; on any product of AT&T, Bass's globe identifies the world's largest industrial complex, which has now been broken up into smaller ones—also bearing his imprint. And what about Celanese and Warner Communications, Minolta, Quaker Oats or a U.S. postage stamp? The list is endless and growing. But here's the best part of it; you walk through that little building on Sunset Boulevard and it looks like a local enterprise—relaxed, quiet, home-like. You could never guess that from this little house come all these milestones of imagery. There are many people busy on their own or with Bass. And in the middle of it all sits Bass behind a desk so cluttered with Pre-Columbian, American Indian and other artifacts, that there's hardly room for his layout pad.

He is on the phone, soft-spoken, with a smile (even in his voice) telling a client the only way to go about it.

1956年春、私はウォルドルフ・アストリアのボールルームで、ニューヨークアートディレクターズクラブから初めて金賞を受賞するため、壇上に向かって並んでいた。とても緊張していた。昼食の間、慣れない靴をテーブルの下で脱いでいたので、名前を呼ばれた時に履くのを忘れてしまった。私はそのまま戻るともできずに、口ひげをたくわえた優しそうな男の後ろに立った。男がとても落ち着いていたので、私は一層緊張した。彼は「人生なんてばかげたものさ」とでもいうような独特の表情で「やあ!」と会釈した。3分後アナウンスが流れ、「黄金の腕」だったと思うが映画のタイトルで彼が受賞したことが告げられた。それがバスとの出会いだった。10年後アスペンデザイン会議で再会したが、それまでに彼の人柄と作品をもっと知ることになった。(身の回りにこれほど多くの作品があるのに、業界で彼を知らないという人がいるだろうか。)

彼の映画タイトルは他にも数多く見てきたが、そのほとんどはオットー・プレミンジャーと激しいやりとりをしながら作りあげた傑作である。その中には私のお気に入りの「荒野を歩け」や「栄光への脱出」、そしてヒッチコックと作った「北北西に進路を取れ」などがある。ヒッチコックとはまた「サイコ」で、有名な恐怖の連続するシャワー殺人場面を展開した。「Why May Creates」という素晴らしい短編映画も監督したが、そこには現実も、出会いの時彼が見せたユーモアも失わない文明が凝縮されている。「グランプリ」のカーレースや「スパルタカス」の戦場など他にもいろいろある。近作映画「クエスト」は妻イレーンとの共同制作で、人生は8日間に凝縮できるという、不思議でシュールな世界を描いた旅物語である。子供が光と自由に通じる不思議なドアへ向かう。レイ・ブラッドベリの台本と(制作費の高い宇宙映画のような陳腐なものではない)シンプルだが複雑な効果は、その青みがかった灰色の世界に神秘的で危険な香りを加える。それは、ほんの数日で大人に成長した子供が自由と長寿を得るという結末の数分と対照的である。

ここまででも一生かかりそうな仕事の量だが、バスの作品はあちちに、世界中に存在する。最近彼とイスラエルの砂漠をドライブし、エッソのガソリンスタンドを通り過ぎた。彼がその基本デザインをしたことを知っていたので顔を見ると彼もうなずいた。ユナイテッド航空の乗り入れる空港に掲げられた「2つのU」。AT&Tの全製品に表示された世界最大の企業を表わす「地球」。AT&Tは分割されたが、後の各社のシンボルも彼がデザインした。このようにバスのデザインを至る所で目にするとは驚くべきことだ。他にもセラニース、ワーナーコミュニケーション、ミノルタ、クウェーカーオーツ、アメリカの切手と挙げればきりがない。

サンセット大通りに面した小さな建物の内部は落ち着いた民家のような雰囲気で、中小企業のように見える。この小さな家から歴史的な名作が生み出されているとは、誰も思わないだろう。中では大勢の人が忙しく働いている。その中央で、バスは有史以前のアメリカインディアンの工芸品などで散らかった、レイアウト用紙を置くスペースもない机に向かっている。そして彼は受話器を手に、おだやかな口調で(声までも)微笑みながら、クライアントに仕事の進め方を説明している。

1 Cover illustration for architectural magazine 建築雑誌の表紙イラストレーション 1992

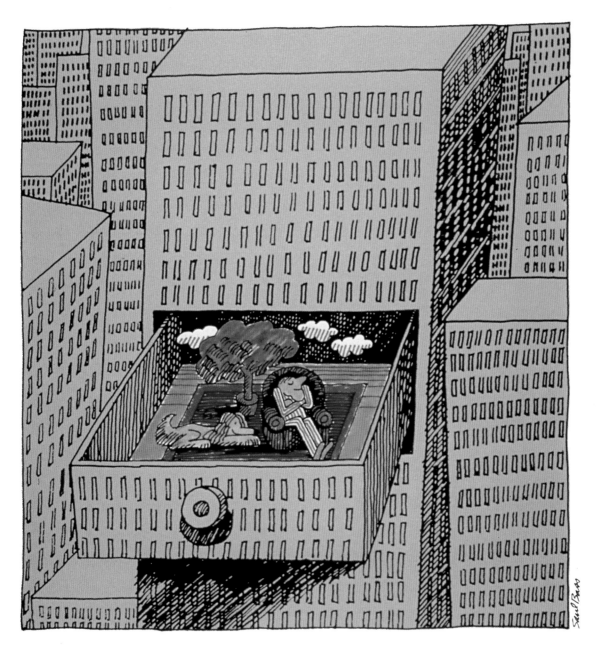

Some of my
Best Friends

Arthur Whitelaw, Jack Schlissel and Leonard Soloway present 'Some of My Best Friends'
A new comedy by Stanley Hart · with Ted Knight · Lee Wallace · Gavin Reed · Alice Drummond
Ralph Williams · Trish Hawkins · Bob Balaban · Associate Producers: Donald Tick and
Martin Markinson · Production Designed by Eugene Lee · Lighting Designed by Ken Billington
Directed by Harold Prince 🌳 Longacre Theatre, West 48th Street, New York

3 Theater poster 演劇ポスター 1977

4

HENRY FONDA, CHARLES LAUGHTON, DON MURRAY, WALTER PIDGEON, PETER LAWFORD, GENE TIERNEY, LEW
AYRES, FRANCHOT TONE, BURGESS MEREDITH, EDDIE HODGES, PAUL FORD, GEORGE GRIZZARD, INGA SWENSON
SCREENPLAY WRITTEN BY WENDELL MAYES, MUSIC BY JERRY FIELDING, PHOTOGRAPHED IN PANAVISION
BY SAM LEAVITT, PRODUCED AND DIRECTED BY OTTO PREMINGER, A COLUMBIA PICTURES RELEASE

6

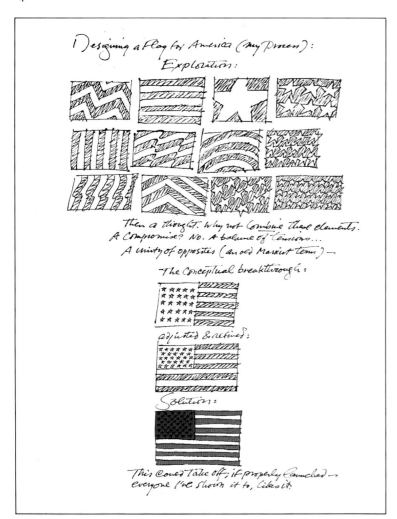

4　Entry solicitation poster　出展募集ポスター　1989
5　Flag design for magazine　雑誌のための旗のデザイン　1972
6　Film poster　映画ポスター　1962

5

THE FIXER

WITH ALAN BATES · DIRECTED BY JOHN FRANKENHEIMER · A JOHN FRANKENHEIMER—EDWARD LEWIS PRODUCTION · AN MGM RELEASE

7 Film poster 映画ポスター 1968

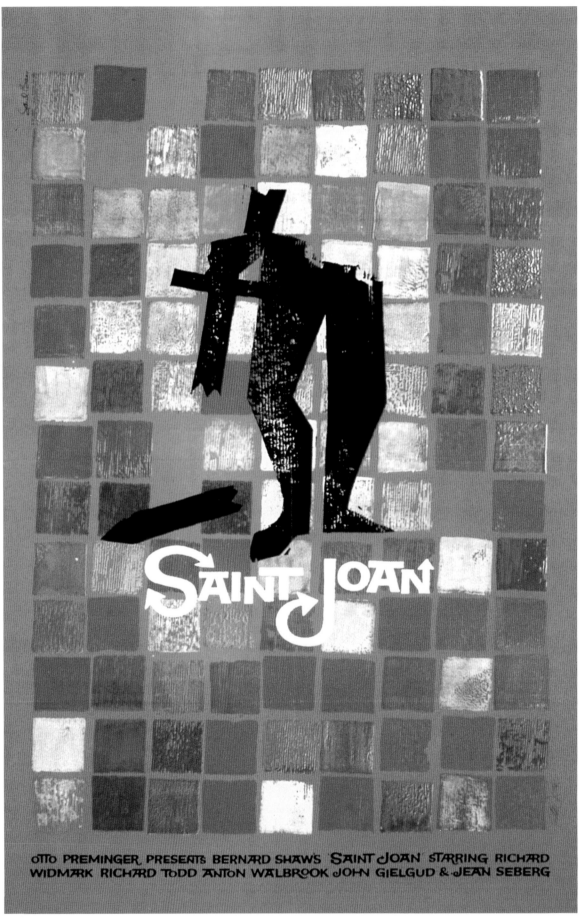

8　Film poster 映画ポスター 1956

"If the book be false in its facts, disprove them; if false in its reasoning, refute it. But, for God's sake, let us freely hear both sides, if we choose." — From a letter by Thomas Jefferson, April 19, 1814.

BETTE DAVIS IN STORM CENTER

watch for this MOTION PICTURE at your local theatre

9 Film poster 映画ポスター 1957

10 Film poster 映画ポスター 1963

11 Film poster 映画ポスター 1966

12 Civil rights poster 市民権ポスター 1975

13　Film symbol　映画のシンボル 1960

14　Film poster　映画ポスター 1960

SUCH GOOD FRIENDS

AN OTTO PREMINGER FILM · DYAN CANNON, JAMES COCO, JENNIFER O'NEILL, KEN HOWARD NINA FOCH, LAURENCE LUCKINBILL, LOUISE LASSER, BURGES MEREDITH, SAM LEVINE, WILLIAM REDFELD · SCREENPLAY, ESTHER DALE BASED ON DAVID SHABER'S ADAPTATION OF THE NOVEL BY LOIS GOULD · MUSIC BY THOMAS Z. SHEPARD · PRODUCED AND DIRECTED BY OTTO PREMINGER

19 Film poster 映画ポスター 1974

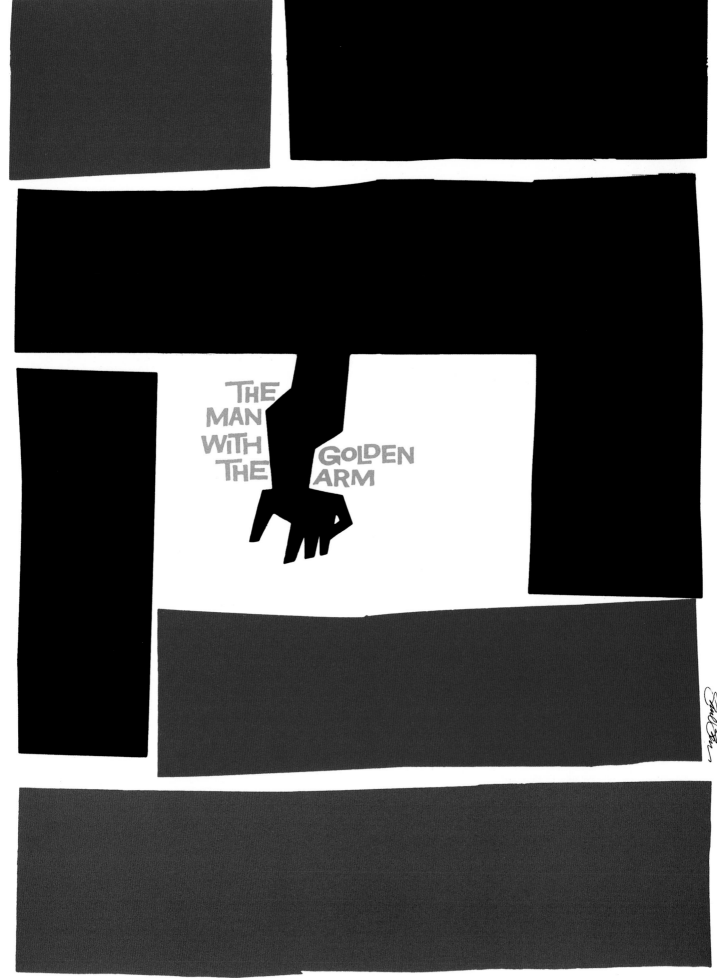

20　Film poster　映画ポスター　1955

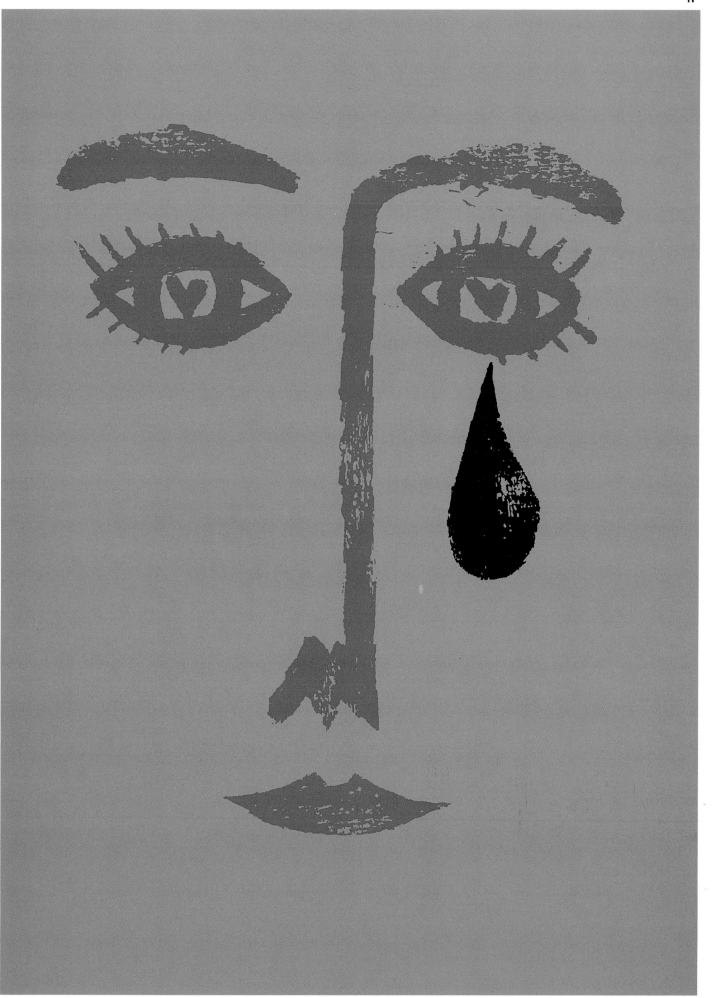

21 Film poster 映画ポスター 1957

8TH SAN FRANCISCO INTERNATIONAL FILM FESTIVAL·OCTOBER 14TH TO 27TH 1964 CORONET THEATRE

22　Film festival poster 映画祭のポスター 1964

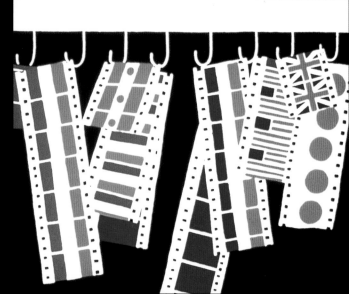

24　Film festival poster 映画祭のポスター 1964

23　Film festival poster 映画祭のポスター 1984

Chicago International Film Festival —

For the Los. Angeles Music Center

28 Poster for concert tour コンサートツアーのポスター 1987

27 Image poster イメージポスター 1986

29 Constitution commemorative poster 憲法制定記念のポスター 1986

30 Exploratory symbols for film 映画のためのシンボル 1980

31 Self-portrait 自画像 1991

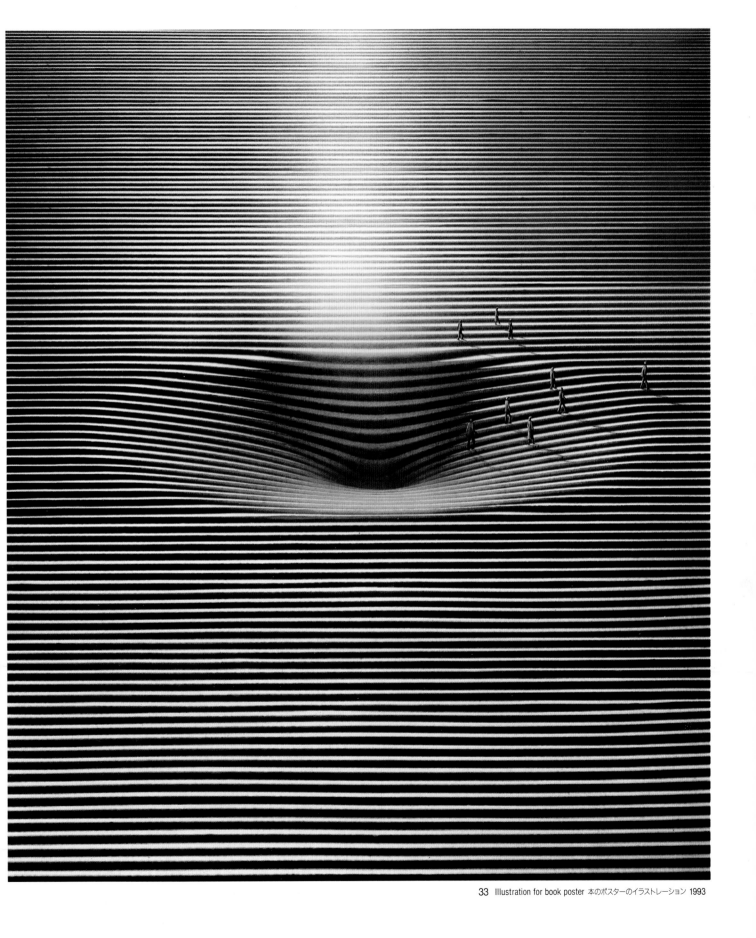

33 Illustration for book poster 本のポスターのイラストレーション 1993

35 Illustration for book cover 本の表紙イラストレーション 1993

BORIS ZABOROV ボリス・ザボロフ Painter

Yusuke Nakahara 中原佑介

Boris Zaborov's paintings contain images that are imbued simultaneously with both a tenacious strength and a temporal evanescence. His images appear at once to be vanishing slowly into darkness, at the same time as they seem to be emerging ever so gradually from out of that darkness. They demonstrate a conflicting duality—being concurrently in both creative and extinctive modes. It is a duality that renders them inherently unstable.

Images in the human memory are strikingly alike. With the passage of time they too grow increasingly vague and uncertain; yet with a reflective pause of recollection they are brought back to life in an instant. It is these instantaneously resuscitated images that Zaborov depicts in his paintings.

Zaborov's paintings are based on photographs. His interest in photography is no doubt an outgrowth of his perception of imagistic duality in this medium as well. On one hand, photographs are in an extinctive mode: over the course of time they gradually change color and lose the sharpness of their detail. (In this case, the transformation is especially marked due to their chemical origin.) On the other hand, any time we look at a photo, we retrieve its fading image and impel it into a creative mode—to form a new image of the instant.

Zaborov takes these instantaneous photographic images and injects them into his paintings. Initially he draws an image on paper or canvas. Next he applies multiple layers of a mixture of acrylic paint and gesso. When this overlay has dried, he sandpapers the surface until the underlying image shows through. It is a process which itself involves the duality of image extinction and creation: the final image can be described as half-rising to the surface or half-hidden below it.

The majority of Zaborov's artistic images are human. In each case his subject is shown facing the camera squarely, with a visible air of nervous tension. They are not casual snapshots, but commemorative portraits. Each bears the imprint of a most unusual aura—the aura, though only so faint, of having experienced something and survived.

Zaborov was born in Minsk, the capital of what was then Belorussia. After studying art at the Minsk Fine Arts School, the St. Petersburg Academy of Fine Arts and the Sourikov Art Institute in Moscow, he pursued a career in book illustration in Minsk for more than twenty years before ultimately emigrating to Paris. Zaborov recalls his feelings in those early days abroad: "Solitude made me more aware of the inner resonance of things. The mysterious process of the intermingling of past and present gave birth in me to the deeply nostalgic state of mind which is at the basis of my work. And so I began to work." Being far from his homeland perhaps awakened him to the temporal evanescence of human memory.

Zaborov is unique, however. No other artist ever came upon the same style. Nor did any other artist ever choose to paint the creative-extinctive duality of imagery. Never before Zaborov, in the long history of contact between photography and painting, had photography assumed the role it does in his work. And nowhere else are photography and painting so intimately intertwined.

ボリス・ザボロフの絵画にはイメージの強靭さとはかなさが共存しているように感じられる。それは暗闇のなかに次第に消え去ってゆくイメージのようでもあり、暗闇から徐々に姿をあらわしつつあるイメージのようにも見える。イメージは生成に向かうと同時に消滅にも向かっているといった二重性を示している。つまり、イメージは不安定なのである。

しかし、人間の記憶するイメージもまた同じことである。それは時の経過とともに不確かなあいまいなものに変わってゆき、イメージを思い出すというのはそれを束の間蘇らせるということに他ならないからだ。ザボロフの絵画はこの束の間のイメージを描いたものだといってもいい。

ボリス・ザボロフは写真をもとにして描いているというが、この画家の写真への関心はまた、同じ事情に根ざしたものではあるまいか。写真は年月を経るにしたがって変色し、ディテイルがぼやけてゆく。それは像の消滅に向かう。化学変化によってつくりだされたイメージだけにその変化はいちじるしい。しかし、その一瞬一瞬に、写真を見るものはそこからイメージを生成し、像を引き出すのである。それは文字通り、束の間のイメージの形成である。

ザボロフの絵画には、写真のこの束の間のイメージが画面に引き入れられている。この画家は紙、あるいはキャンバスにイメージを描き、その上にアクリル絵具とジェッソを混ぜたものを何回も塗り、それが固まったあと、表面を紙やすりでこすって最初に描いたイメージを浮き出させるという手法を採っているという。この技法自体、イメージの消去と生成という二重性を物語っている。こすり出されたイメージは浮き出ているともいえるし、なかば隠されているともいえるからである。

イメージはその大半が人物像である。人物はいずれもカメラに向かって身構えて、緊張した面持ちをしている。スナップではなく、記念写真的である。そして、それらの人物にはある独特なオーラのようなものが感じられる。ささやかであれなにかを体験してきたその余波のようなものが。

ザボロフは旧白ロシアの首都ミンスクに生れ、同市の美術学校、サンクトペテルブルグの美術アカデミー、モスクワのスリコフ美術学校を経たのち、故郷のミンスクで長いあいだ本の挿絵の仕事に従事し、20年を経たのち故国を離れパリへ移住したという経歴の持主である。「孤独は事物との内面的な共鳴に敏感にさせた。過去と現在を混在させるふしぎなプロセスが、私の底深いノスタルジックな心のなかに生れ、それが私の仕事の基礎となった。そして私は制作を始めた。」ザボロフはこう回想しているが、故国を遠く離れたことが、記憶のはかなさに目覚めさせたのかもしれない。

しかし、他のどの画家もこういうスタイルを見出さなかった。イメージのもつ生成と消滅の二重性を絵画にしなかった。写真と絵画の接触の歴史は古いが、写真がこういうかたちで絵画に登場したことはなかった。絵画と写真のもっとも深い次元での相互浸透がここにはある。

1 "The Horse" 「馬」 1983

2 "House in the Country"「田舎の別荘」1986

3 "The Little Landscape"「小風景」1987

4 "Cart" 「荷馬車」 1986

5 "Young Man Holding a Hat" 「帽子を持った青年」 1986

63

6 "A Family"「家族」1987

7 "Girl with Flowers in Her Hair"「花飾りをつけた少女」1986

8 "Woman with Children" 「子供たちと女」 1986

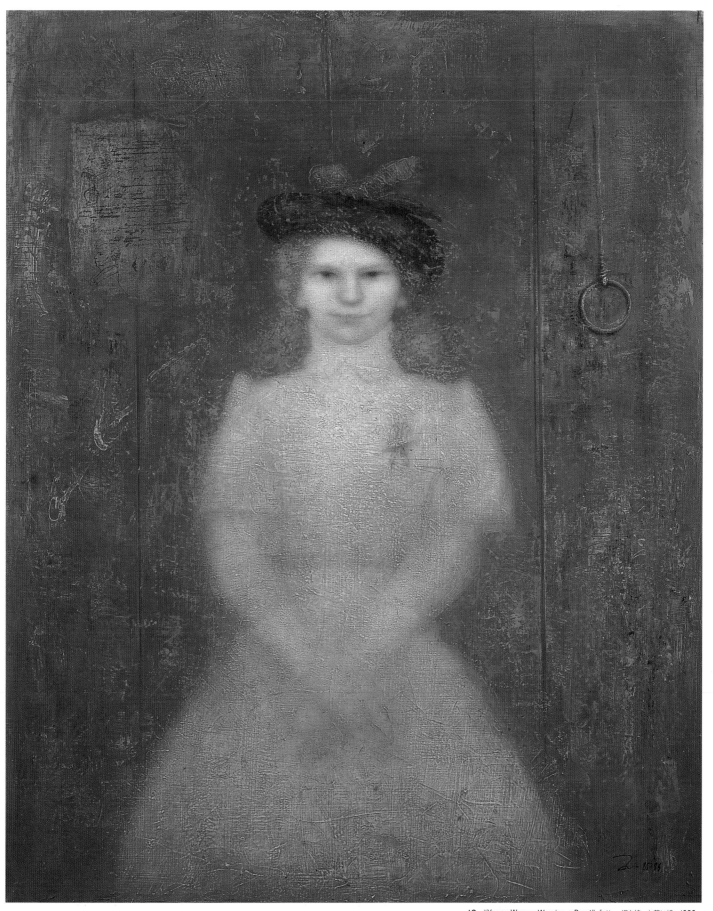

12 "Young Woman Wearing a Beret" 「ベレー帽を被った若い娘」 1986

13　"Girl with Racket"「ラケットを持った少女」1985

15 "Girl with Dog"「犬を連れた娘」1981

14 "Children Holding Hands"「手をつなぐ二人の子供」1986

16 "Little Girl with Doll"「人形を持つ少女」1986

17 "Serious Young Girl" 「手を組む娘」1986

18 "Housewife"「主婦」1990

19 "Two Figures in Landscape"「風景の中の二人の人物」1989

20 "A Girl at Table"「テーブルの娘」1990

21 "The Blue Square" 「青い正方形」1989

22 "Lying Nude" 「横たわる裸婦」1989

23 "Nude in Garden"「庭にいる裸婦」1989

24 "Vania and Aphrodite" 「ヴァニアとアフロデーテー」 1989

25 "Dialogue" 「対話」1989

AKIRA SETO 瀬戸 照

Hiroshi Kojitani 麹谷 宏

I recently had the opportunity to view a large number of highly detailed, weird drawings—originals. What made them "weird" was their depiction of a world of death and silence: plants and insects and fruit all shriveled up and decayed. Mingled with these were large quantities of fossils, mineral specimens, chips of stone and the like, creating a most unusual and nihilistic mood. The drawings were surprisingly small, almost the actual size of real insects and rocks. What struck me as particularly strange was the way in which these finely detailed works, despite their withered portrayals, exuded an aura of powerful strength. It was as though they were imbued with a hidden capacity of movement, so much so, that one would be tempted to describe them as vibrantly alive.

I was flabbergasted to learn that the drawings were the work of Akira Seto. I was taken aback because I was well familiar with Seto's illustrations, since he was an old friend and frequent collaborator of my design partner, Kensuke Irie. On many occasions I had taken note of Seto's vivid flower illustrations or other vivacious works on Irie's desk, and I had long assumed that he was an artist who drew only things of beauty. Hence my great astonishment to discover that this same individual was also producing exquisite requiems of death and devastation, and with so observant and loving an eye. How, I wondered, could such inherent opposites—life vs. death, positive vs. negative, the kinetic vs. the static—coexist in one artist's creative soul?

Being the insuppressibly curious person that I am, I decided to visit Seto's studio to find out. His studio, I discovered, was filled with an aura of stoic silence. Realizing the incredible amount of time—and effort—which Seto must spend in this isolated chamber to produce his style of work, I surmised that he probably isn't very fond of drawing subjects which are alive and changing. Living subjects change too rapidly for Seto, an artist whose creative process involves observation, more observation and further observation. If he draws an apple, for example, by the time he finishes just half his drawing, the apple itself has already gone rotten. The final portrait thus turns out as an unlikely piece of fruit with one half glowingly fresh and the other half pitifully shriveled. A drawing precisely of this kind hangs in Seto's studio.

Since he is also a commercial artist, Seto of course has the knowhow to get a job done on a tight schedule. As might be expected, however, he finds such work too rushed and therefore not very satisfying. So when he undertakes work of his own choosing for an exhibition or such, he invariably opts for subjects that wilt in the course of his lengthy observations—subjects that ultimately reach the static state he so much prefers, a state which he repeatedly described to me as "true beauty."

Seto's drawings, though static depictions, are by no means evocations of mere realism, however. On close scrutiny they reveal coloration and expression different from the real object. Also, though the subjects he draws are physically dead, they are not dead in his drawings. This is surely because the objects continue to live in his mind's eye. He draws them as he remembers them, adding his own loving touch along the way. It is for this reason that Seto's works are, indeed, vibrantly alive.

瀬戸には、おどろかされた。

先月、不思議な超精密画の原画をたくさん見る機会があった。不思議というのは、そこに描かれているのは、まるで死と静寂の世界——植物も昆虫も果実もすべて、枯れ落ち朽ち果てたものばかりなのだ。そしてこれにまじって、数多くの化石、鉱物標本、岩石片などが虚無的な姿を並べて独特の雰囲気を漂わせていた。

それらの原画は意外に小さく、ほとんど化石や昆虫の原寸大で描かれている。ところが、その精緻なタッチで表現されている枯れ萎んだものたちの表情には、不思議に愛情のある熱っぽい力強さがあり、動きを秘めたような存在感も感じられて、朽ち果てたものを描いているにもかかわらず、なぜか「生き生きとした」という言葉で説明したくなるほどに魅力的なものだった。この作品が、瀬戸照のものと聞いておどろいたのだった。

というのは、瀬戸は、ぼくのデザイン・パートナー入江健介の古い友人で、共作も多い。だから入江の机に時々載っている瀬戸の、みずみずしいシズル感にあふれたくだものや、ヴィヴィッドな美しさに満ちた花のイラストレーションなどは、よく目にして知っていた。その同じ、美しいものしか描かないと思っていたアーチストが、枯れ死に、朽ち果ててゆくものたちの姿に、これほどの愛情あふれる目くばりで精美なレクイエムを描きおくっているとは。

陰と陽、動と静、生と死——いったい、この共存できないはずのものが、一人のアーチストの心の中をどう住み分けているのだろう。人一倍好奇心の強いぼくとしては、もうこうなると瀬戸のアトリエをのぞかずにはおさまらなくなっていた。

ストイックで静かなアトリエの空間。この小さな密室の中の、気の遠くなるような制作の手数と濃密な時間にふれて気がついたのだが、瀬戸はたぶん、生きていて変化しているものは、あまり描きたくないのだと思う。描写対象を観察し、観察し、観察し続けながら描く瀬戸の制作時間の中では、生きているものの変化は速すぎて、例えば、左側から描きはじめたリンゴが右側を描くころにはもう腐っているという、ウソのような事態となる。ウソではない証拠に、そのまま描き続けた「時間差リンゴ」の絵がアトリエに掛かっている。

もちろん、瀬戸はコマーシャルな仕事もするから、それなりのノウ・ハウは持ってはいるが（なかなかにユニーク）、そういう制作はやはりあわただしくて、あまり幸せではないらしい。だから、描く対象を自由に選べる仕事や展覧会のための作品には、長い長い観察ののちに枯れ朽ち果てて、やっと自分の思うように静止してくれたものたちを、（その姿こそ美しいと瀬戸は何度もいった）愛しみながら想いを込めて描きはじめるというわけなのである。

しかし、瀬戸の絵は、静止してしまったものを描きながら、見くらべてみるとわかるのだが、決して単純な写実ではない。かたちを写しながら、実は色も表情も違っているのである。物理的には死んだものを描きながら、瀬戸の絵の中では死んではいないのだ。

それは、あくなき観察の果てに静止してしまったものたちの姿が、瀬戸の視空間の記憶の中では生き続けていて、瀬戸はその表情を自在に描き込みながら、彼らと共有した長い時間の想い出を楽しんでいるからに違いないと思う。

瀬戸の「静止したものたち」の絵には、だからやはり「生き生きとした」という表現が正しいのだろう。

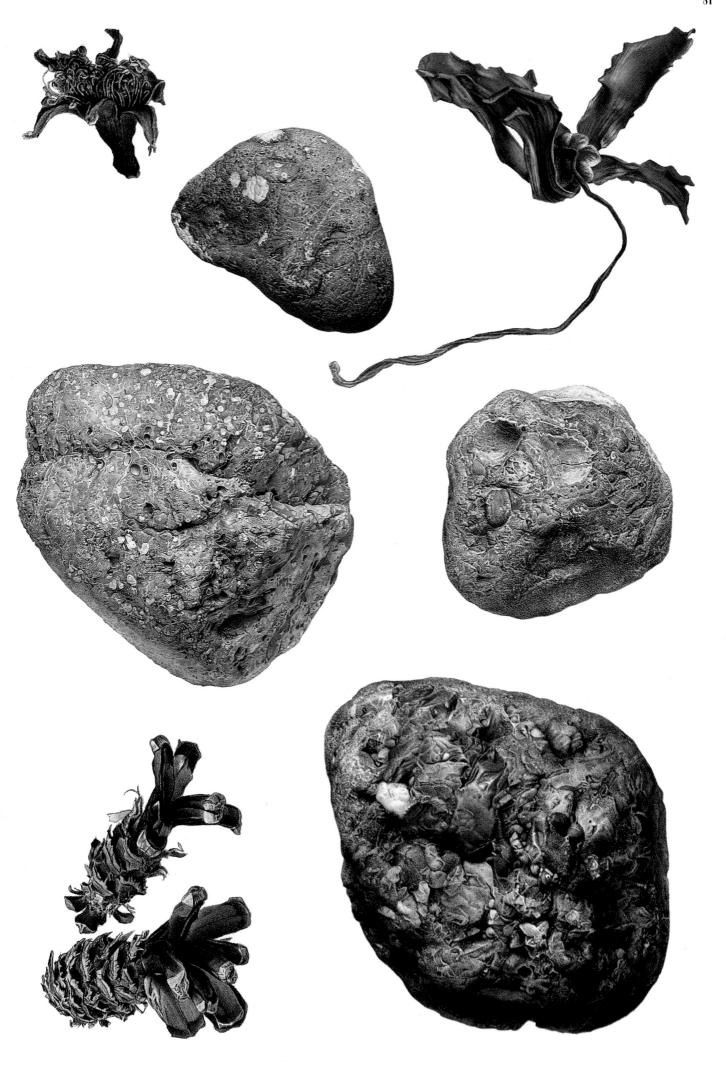

HERB LUBALIN & LOU DORFSMAN ハーブ・ルバリン & ルウ・ドーフスマン

Steven Heller スティーブン・ヘラー

Few graphic designers embody the aesthetics of their times as completely as Herb Lubalin. From the 1950s to 1970s he *was* American graphic design, and "Lubalinesque" was the way to describe a pervasive sensibility that informed the advertising, editorial and package design of the era. He helped build the bridge between Modernism and eclecticism, joining two contrasting methodologies in the service of commerce. He was the master of conceptual typography making letters speak and words emote. He was the pioneer of phototypography, one of its earliest users—and some critics say abusers—who promoted that anti-canonical practice of smashing and overlapping letters. He liberated white space from the ideologues by refusing to follow the edicts of a "less is more" design philosophy. Indeed, for Lubalin more was certainly better as long as it served its purpose. He was a tireless experimenter, whose once radical approaches to type and page design became so thoroughly accepted that it's hard to imagine that Lubalin did not always represent the design canon.

Lubalin had a unique impact on the practice of American and European graphic design for a generation or more. My introduction came in the late 1960s, early in my career, through exposure to two remarkable magazines, each benchmarks of Sixties American culture, and each a model on which I based my own practice: *Eros* and *Avant Garde*. The former, America's first unexpurgated celebration of erotica, was the most elegant example of magazine pacing and composition at the time, regardless of its racy content. The latter, an expression of the social and cultural flux within American society as influenced by the antiwar movement and alternative culture, was a hybrid that crossed a magazine with literary journal. It was square, the size of a record album, and contained graphics that evoked the revolutionary spirit.

Lubalin's typography was rarely neutral. Though he was soft-spoken, in fact almost painfully shy when addressing strangers, he spoke loudly through his work. His headlines for articles and advertisements were stop signs that forced the reader to halt, read and experience before being engrossed by the message. Story titles were tweaked and manipulated to give Lubalin just the right amount of words or letters to make an effective composition. The graphic strength of "No More War," originally an advertisement for *Avant Garde* which features block letters forming the pattern of an American flag with a bold black exclamation point at the end, became one of the most iconographic visual statements issued during the Vietnam War.

Over a decade since his death, it seems that graphic design, and experimentation in general, has taken a sharper turn toward illegibility in the service of profundity. While Lubalin pushed the limits, sometimes beyond the ken of his contemporaries, he rarely went over the edge. With few exceptions his experiments were conducted under marketplace conditions which at once provided certain safeguards and made taking liberties all the more difficult. Lubalin's was not design for design, but design for communication. Even his most radical ideas never strayed from that course. While today it is difficult to think of Lubalin as a young Turk, he was the quintessential rule basher. If not for him, American graphic design would not have become the fine commercial art it is today.

ハーブ・ルバリンほど時代の美を体現するグラフィックデザイナーは少ない。1950年代から70年代にかけて、彼こそがアメリカのグラフィックデザインであり、「ルバリン調」といえば当時の広告、エディトリアルパッケージのデザインの特徴となった、広く普及した感性を表す。彼はコマーシャルのなかで、モダニズムと折衷主義という2つの対照的な方法論を組み合わせ、その橋渡しをした。また、概念的なタイポグラフィーの名手であり、文字に語らせ、言葉に感情を表現させた。写植を早い時期に用いたパイオニアであると同時に、文字を壊したり重ねたりと正統的でない試みをしたため、評論家によっては「文字の乱用者」とも言われた。デザイン哲学では「少ないほどよい」といわれる余白も自由に使った。ルバリンにしてみれば、目的にかなっている限り、余白は多い方が良かったのである。文字やエディトリアルでの新しい試みは、一時は過激に見られても、後にはすっかり受け入れられたので、今日では彼がデザインの主流になかったとは想像しがたい。

ルバリンは欧米のグラフィックデザイン界で、長い間多大な衝撃を与えた。彼の作品を知ったのは、私がこの世界に入った1960年代後半のこと。60年代のアメリカ文化の象徴であり、私自身の仕事の模範ともなった『エロス』と『アヴァンギャルド』という2冊の優れた雑誌によってである。アメリカで初めてエロスを無修整で賛美した雑誌『エロス』は、内容のきわどさにかかわらず、全体の流れといい構成といい当時最も上品な雑誌であった。『アヴァンギャルド』は、アメリカの反戦運動やカウンターカルチャーの影響による社会や文化の変動を表現した、雑誌と文芸誌を合わせたようなものだった。その正方形でLPジャケット大の雑誌には、革命的な精神を喚起する写真や絵が掲載された。

ルバリンのタイポグラフィにはあいまいさといったものがほとんどない。彼は穏やかな話し方をし、初対面の時など痛々しいほどの恥ずかしがり屋だったが、作品を通じて声を大にして主張した。彼の作った記事や広告の見出し文字は、メッセージ以前に読者を引き止め、読ませ、感じさせる一時停止の標識のようなものである。小説のタイトルは、効果的なデザインになるよう単語や文字に手が加えられている。『アヴァンギャルド』に掲載する広告として作られた"No More War!"は、星条旗を模した文字のかたまりと、後ろの太く黒い感嘆符で構成されているが、これはベトナム戦争下で発せられた、最も印象的な視覚表現のひとつとなった。

彼の死から10年以上経つが、グラフィックデザインだけでなく新しい表現全般が、深遠な意味を追求した結果分かりにくい方向へと急転した。ルバリンは表現の限界を広げ、当時の人々の理解を越えることはあっても、行き過ぎることはほとんどなかった。彼のデザインはデザインのためのデザインではなく、コミュニケーションのためのデザインであった。その最も過激な発想も、コミュニケーションという目的からそれることはなかった。今日では想像しがたいが、彼は生粋の規則破りだった。もしそうでなかったなら、アメリカのグラフィックデザインは、これほど素晴らしいアートにはなっていなかっただろう。

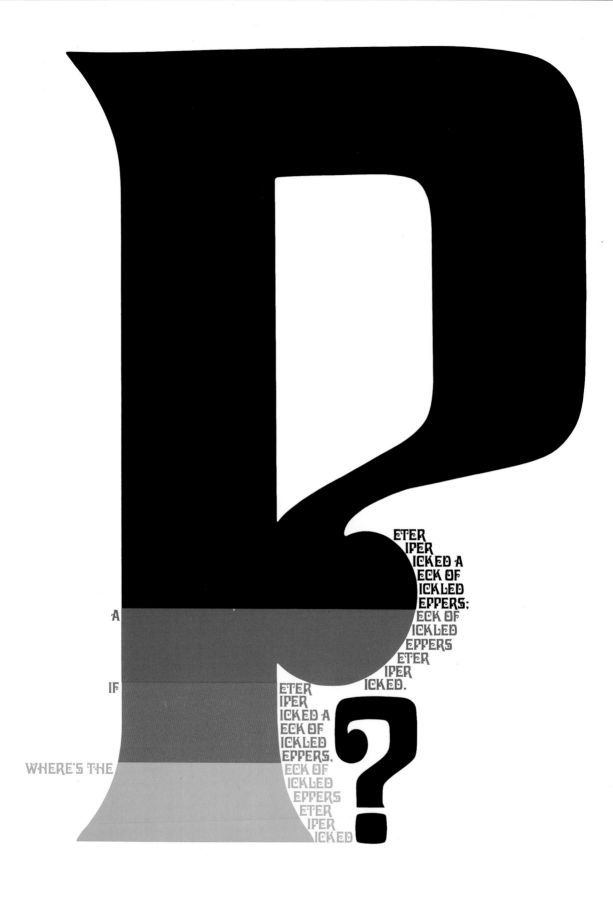

1965 NATIONAL TYPE FACE DESIGN COMPETITION AWARD WINNING TYPE FACE: LINCOLN GOTHIC BY THOMAS W. LINCOLN / SPONSORED BY: VISUAL GRAPHICS CORPORATION (MANUFACTURER OF THE PHOTO TYPOSITOR) / POSTER DESIGN: HERB LUBALIN / TYPOSITOR TYPOGRAPHY: AARON BURNS & COMPANY, DIVISION OF RAPID TYPOGRAPHERS, INC / SILK SCREEN: M H. LAVORE COMPANY INC.

2   Poster for typesetting company 写植会社のポスター

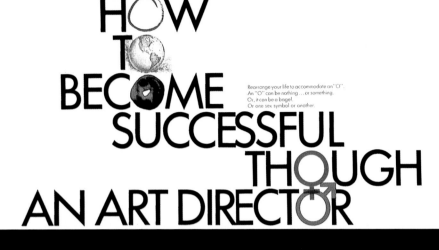

HOW TO BECOME SUCCESSFUL THOUGH AN ART DIRECTOR

Rearrange your life to accommodate an "O".
An "O" can be nothing . . . or something.
Or, it can be a bagel.
Or one sex symbol or another.

3

HOW TO BECOME SUCCESSFUL THOUGH AN ART DIRECTOR

An "O" can mean money.
Money talks.
A successful career is often built on a sound foundation of it.
Set your sights on this valuable commodity.

4

HOW TO BECOME $UCCE$$FUL THOUGH AN ART DIRECTOR

Yours.
All yours.
To own.
To cherish.
To prize.
To encase in plastic.

Forever.

5

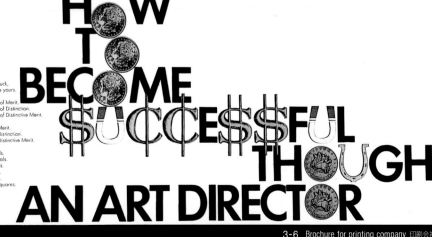

HOW TO BECOME $UCCE$$FUL THOUGH AN ART DIRECTOR

So,
achieve.
And,
with a little luck,
glory can be yours.
Certificates.
Certificates of Merit.
Certificates of Distinction.
Certificates of Distinctive Merit.
Awards.
Awards of Merit.
Awards of Distinction.
Awards of Distinctive Merit.
Medals.
Silver medals.
Bronze medals.
Gold medals.
Gold Cleos.
Gold Andys.
Golden T-Squares.
Etc.

3-6 Brochure for printing company 印刷会社のパンフレット

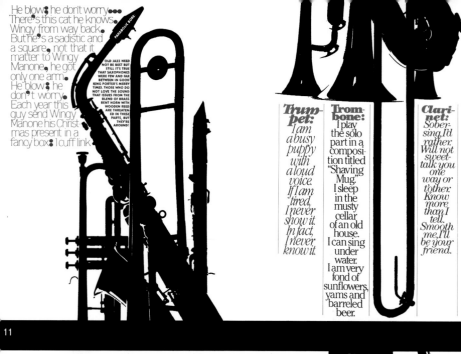

He blow; he don't worry... There's this cat he knows. Wingy from way back. But he's a sadistic and a square, not that it matter to Wingy Manone; he got only one arm. He blow; he don't worry. Each year this guy send Wingy Manone his Christmas present in a fancy box: 1 cuff link.

OLD JAZZ NEED NOT BE BEST BUT STILL IT'S TRUE THAT SAXOPHONES WERE FEW AND FAR BETWEEN IN GOOD KING PORTER'S MERRY TIMES. THOSE WHO DO NOT LOVE THE SOUND THAT ISSUES FROM THE BLEND OF BRASS BENT HORN WITH WOODEN REED ARE THREATENED IN THESE PARTS, BUT THEY'RE AROUND!

Trumpet: I am a busy puppy with a loud voice. If I am tired, I never show it. In fact, I never know it.

Trombone: I play the solo part in a composition titled "Shaving Mug." I sleep in the musty cellar of an old house. I can sing under water. I am very fond of sunflowers, yams and barreled beer.

Clarinet: Sober sing, I'd rather. Will not sweet-talk you one way or t'other. Know more than I tell. Smooth me, I'll be your friend.

"CHECK YOU AT LINGA LONGA."

We made it over the Jefferson Davis Highway in a Model-T some 200 miles south of Richmond, Virginia, in the State of North Carolina, a couple of 18-year-old kids. The back of the open touring car was loaded with ponchos, pup tents, army blankets and cans of Van Camp's pork and beans. I had a pen knife that was an arsenal in the pocket: two cutting blades, a can-opener, a bottle-opener and a corkscrew. I'd never before in my life been south of Philadelphia nor heard of Brunswick stew. The girls walking along Fayetville Street were unbelievable. Corn silk, they made me think of. I could not take my eyes off them. Were these the southern belles I had read about? That night, we saw Norma Talmadge, Conway Tearle and Wallace Beery in "Ashes of Vengeance" at the Superba Theatre, college kids in the audience, hissing the villain. The next day was Saturday and in the afternoon my Carolina cousin Fed (short for Confederate), two of his school friends and the two of us piled into the Ford and went checkin'. Checkin' was riding up and down the wide street bordering the campus as the girls either sat on the lawn or promenaded within limits. On Saturday afternoon, everybody went checkin' mainly to arrange for more checkin' later on. "Check you at Linga Longa," one of the boys called out to a honey blonde. Linga Longa, seemed to be the place. That's what they kept saying: Linga Longa. Saturday night, we put on our white pants and blue blazers and drove through cotton fields and scrub pine to Linga Longa. But the sign said Linger Longer. Southern talk had thrown me. Linger Longer was a kind of lake resort featuring an out-door dance pavilion in a pine grove. The floor was jammed with dancers and boys cutting in, the first I ever saw of that practice. Band was a piano, trumpet, trombone, clarinet, banjo, drums—Negro musicians. "Ja Da," familiar since World War One, was the old-shoe favorite: Ja da, Ja da, jada jada jing jing, jing...a strain, really, like so many great jazz vehicles. Then "Sister Kate" did her shimmy, "Wang Wang Blues" cut out, followed by "Indiana" and "Everybody Loves My Baby but My Baby Loves Nobody but Me." Six of us on the way home in the Model-T, and check in achieved its objective of neckin'. At eighteen, we'd already won the grand prize: full possession of the hour. Did I dream all this?

LASTING LESSONS TAUGHT IN RHYTHM

...OF HEAVEN: SO HIGH, CAN'T GET OVER IT;

SO LOW, CAN'T GET UNDER IT; SO WIDE, CAN'T GET AROUND IT; YOU MUST COME IN AT THE DOOR.

...OF EARTH: NOBODY WANTS YOU WHEN YOU'RE DOWN AND OUT!

...OF MAMIE'S SINS AND SORROWS: IF YOU CAN'T GIVE A DOLLAR, GIVE ME A LOUSY DIME. I WANNA FEED THAT HUNGRY MAN OF MINE.

Über die Philosophie der Kunst.

An evening in the year of 1935. Huebner's garden restaurant in the Stadtpark, Vienna.

It's Spring, 2 American young men are seated at a table drinking Kaffee mit Schlag. The band is playing the Saint James Infirmary Blues.

1ST AMER: NOT BAD.
2ND AMER: NOT GOOD, EITHER.
1ST AMER: GIVE THEM A CHANCE; THEY'LL GET IT.
2ND AMER: THE DRUMMER KNOWS THE TRICKS. HE MUST HAVE STUDIED.
1ST AMER: YOU'VE GOT TO STUDY.
2ND AMER: AND YOU'VE GOT TO FORGET YOU STUDIED. JAZZ DRUMMER LIKE BABY DODDS, CHICK WEBB, COZY COLE, HE GIVES YOU THAT MOVE-ALONG FEELING.
1ST AMER: I GUESS THAT'S IT; THAT MOVE-ALONG FEELING.
2ND AMER: THAT'S NOT ALL; YOU'VE GOT TO PASS THE TEST.
1ST AMER: WHAT IS THE TEST?
2ND AMER: THE TEST OF A JAZZ DRUMMER IS: CAN HE MAKE A FAT MAN FALL DOWN A WHOLE FLIGHT OF STAIRS WITHOUT HURTING HIMSELF.

ETIENNE DELESSERT FOREWORD BY JEAN PIAGET

HOW

THE MOUSE
WAS HIT ON
THE HEAD BY A
STONE AND SO
DISCOVERED
THE WORLD

HARRIS
WOULFE
LEWINE
137 EAST
36 STREET
NY 10016
OR 96839

Castro's Cuba, Cuba's Fidel

A JAZZ LEXICON

READY TO RIOT

Memoirs of a Bullfighter

Ford: The Dust and the Glory

HARLEM ON MY MIND

JAZZMASTERS OF THE 40's

THE GLORY OF THEIR TIMES

The Progress of the Protestant

PORTAL TO AMERICA

The De-Romanization of the American Catholic Church

Lytton Strachey

An Editorial, Art Direction, and Packaging Service to the Trade.

15 Letterhead レターヘッド

THIRTY DAYS
HATH
SEPTEMBER,
APRIL,
JUNE,
AND
NOVEMBER;
ALL THE
REST
HAVE
THIRTY-
ONE,

EXCEPT FEBRUARY
AND THAT
HAS
TWENTY-EIGHT
DAYS
CLEAR
AND TWENTY-NINE
IN
EACH
LEAP
YEAR.

16 Design for calendar page カレンダーのためのデザイン

17 Logotype for city of New York ニューヨーク市のロゴタイプ

18 Logotype for magazine 雑誌のロゴタイプ

19 Logotype for news agency 通信社のロゴタイプ

20 Logotype ロゴタイプ

21 Logotype for typesetting company 写植会社のロゴタイプ

24 Christmas card クリスマスカード

22 Logotype for manufacturer of paint brushes 絵筆メーカーのロゴタイプ

23 Logotype for interior design firm インテリアデザイン会社のロゴタイプ

25 Logotype for combined broadcast from major networks 3大ネットワーク合同放送のロゴタイプ

26 Thematic treatment for magazine design exhibition 雑誌デザイン展のためのチラシのロゴの処理

27 Logotype for theatrical company 劇団のロゴタイプ

28 Logotype ロゴタイプ

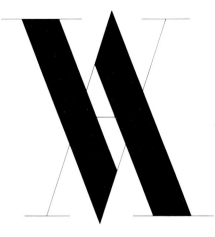

29 Logotype for photographer 写真家のロゴタイプ

30 Logotype for advertising agency 広告代理店のロゴタイプ

31 Logotype for business equipment firm ビジネス機器会社のロゴタイプ

32 Poster announcing design competition デザインコンペの告知ポスター 1964

33 Design for magazine article 雑誌記事のデザイン

34 Announcement for new office opening 新オフィス開設の通知 1964

35 Announcement for exhibition 展覧会の通知

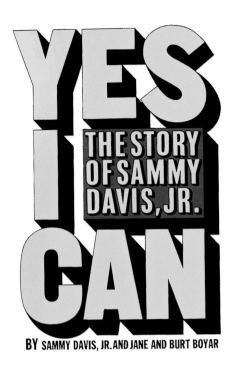

YES I CAN

THE STORY OF SAMMY DAVIS, JR.

CAN

BY SAMMY DAVIS, JR. AND JANE AND BURT BOYAR

36 Book jacket 本の表紙

38 Political poster 政治ポスター

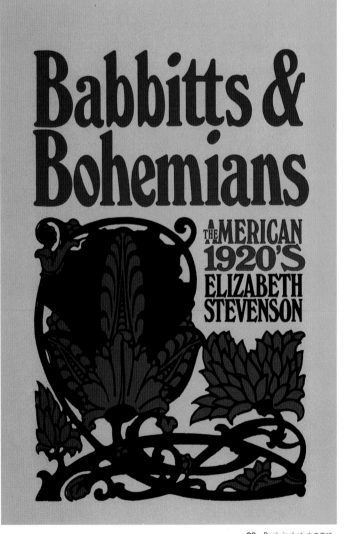

37 Book jacket 本の表紙

39 Book jacket 本の表紙

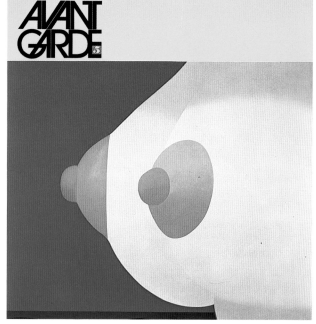

40

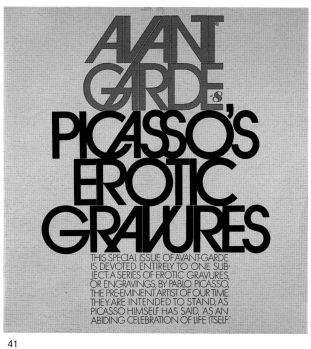

41

43

44

45

"MEN WOULD RATHER HAVE THEIR FILL OF SLEEP, LOVE, AND SINGING AND DANCING THAN OF WAR," SAID HOMER. THE EDITORS OF AVANT-GARDE AGREE, AND DO HEREBY ISSUE A CALL FOR ENTRIES FOR AN INTERNATIONAL POSTER COMPETITION BASED ON THE THEME:

NO MORE WAR!

Judges: Richard Avedon, Leonard Baskin, Alexander Calder, Milton Glaser, Art Kane, Jack Levine, Herb Lubalin, Dwight Macdonald, Robert Motherwell, Robert Osborn, Larry Rivers, Ben Shahn, Edward Steichen & Sloan Wilson.

THE RULES OF THE CONTEST ARE AS FOLLOWS: All professional painters, designers, illustrators, photographers, cartoonists, and other graphic artists are eligible. Amateurs may enter, too, but only after elimination contests at colleges, art and photography schools, museums, and similar institutions.

Ten winners will be selected. All winning posters will be reproduced and sold for $1 each through bookstores, art supply shops, coffeehouses, boutiques, and similar retail outlets. Sales will be promoted by vigorous advertising and publicity campaigns. Profits will be donated to peace causes as designated by the judges.

Artists will receive a 10% royalty on sales. Advances totaling $1,400 will be presented as follows: $500 to a grand prize-winner and $100 to each of the other nine winners.

All winning posters will be featured in an issue of Avant-Garde Magazine. Fifty of the best entries will be exhibited at a New York museum or gallery and sent on tour of the United States.

Choice of subject matter is at the discretion of individual artists (though posters must bear some relationship to the theme of the contest, world peace). Posters may carry any related slogan, caption, or title—or none at all—and may relate to specific conflicts, such as the war in Vietnam. Entries will be judged on the basis of artistic merit and impact of anti-war message.

Judging will take place in New York on May 30, 1968, Memorial Day. Winners will be announced at a press conference held immediately thereafter.

Deadline is 5 p.m., Monday, May 27, 1968. Entries may not exceed 19" x 25" in size and must be accompanied by artist's name and address.

The address of Avant-Garde, both for entries and inquiries, is 110 W. 40th St., New York, N.Y. 10018, U.S.A.

LEGAL STIPULATIONS: This contest is a non-profit undertaking. All revenues remaining from sales of posters after payment of royalties and out-of-pocket expenses will be donated to peace causes as designated by the judges. Financial records will be audited by certified public accountants. Avant-Garde will exercise all possible care in the handling of entries but assumes no responsibility for loss or damage. Avant-Garde reserves the right to change contest rules or cancel the contest entirely for any reason whatsoever. © 1967 by Avant-Garde.   PRINTED IN U.S.A.

47 Logotype ロゴタイプ

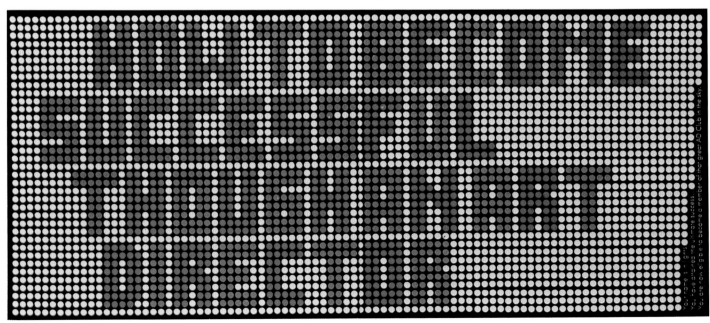

48 Brochure for printing company 印刷会社のパンフレット

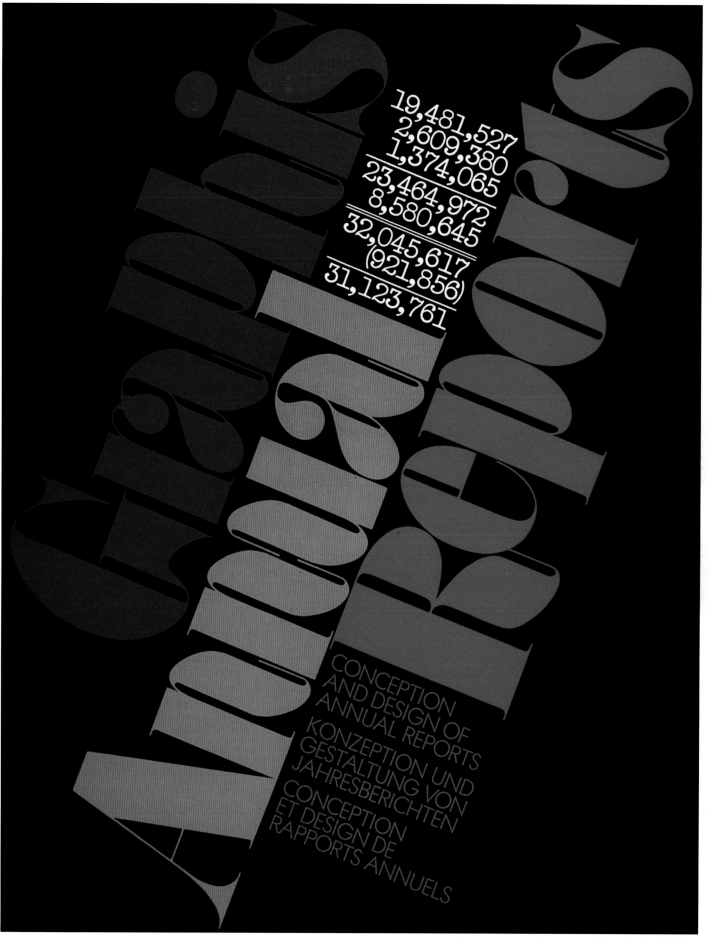

Graphis Annual Reports

19,481,527
2,609,380
1,374,065
23,464,972
8,580,645
32,045,617
(921,856)
31,123,761

CONCEPTION
AND DESIGN OF
ANNUAL REPORTS
KONZEPTION UND
GESTALTUNG VON
JAHRESBERICHTEN
CONCEPTION
ET DESIGN DE
RAPPORTS ANNUELS

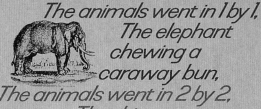

The animals went in 1 by 1,
The elephant
chewing a
caraway bun,
The animals went in 2 by 2,
The rhinoceros
and the
kangaroo,
The animals went in 3 by 3,
The bear,
the flea and the
bumble bee,
The animals went in 4 by 4,
Old Noah got mad
and hollered
for more,
The animals went in 5 by 5,
With Saratoga trunks
they did
arrive,
The animals went in 6 by 6,
The hyena
laughed at the
monkey's tricks,
The animals went in 7 by 7,
Said the ant
to the elephant,
who are you a-shovin'?
The animals went in 8 by 8,
They came with
a rush 'cause 'twas
so late,
The animals went in 9 by 9,
Old Noah
shouted,
"Cut that line!"
The animals went in 10 by 10,
The Ark
she blew her
whistle then.

1965 NATIONAL TYPE FACE DESIGN COMPETITION AWARD WINNING TYPE FACE: EMPHASIS BY ROBERT S. MAILE, JR. / SPONSORED BY: VISUAL GRAPHICS CORPORATION (MANUFACTURER OF THE PHOTO TYPOSITOR) / POSTER DESIGN: HERB LUBALIN / TYPOSITOR TYPOGRAPHY: AARON BURNS & COMPANY, DIVISION OF RAPID TYPOGRAPHICS, INC. / PRINTING: DRUM LITHOGRAPHERS, INC.

WOMEN IN THE KIBBUTZ

LIONEL TIGER & JOSEPH SHEPHER

51 Book jacket 本の表紙

52 Packaging design for cigarette たばこのパッケージデザイン

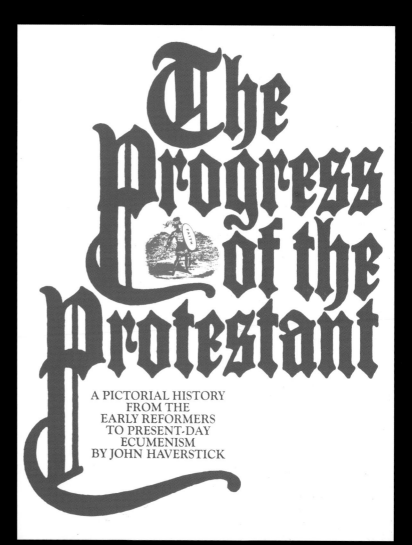

The Progress of the Protestant

A PICTORIAL HISTORY
FROM THE
EARLY REFORMERS
TO PRESENT-DAY
ECUMENISM
BY JOHN HAVERSTICK

53 Book jacket 本の表紙

THIRTY DAYS HATH SEPTEMBER (),

Fair summer gently fades away,
And withering flowers fortel her doom,
Thus will earth's brightest joys decay,
And bear us with them to the tomb.

APRIL (),JUNE AND ()

Though Nature smiles when comes her time,
And decks the fields in verdant green,
Yet in our cold New England clime
Few pleasant days this month are seen.

Fair Summer reigns o'er all the land-
How mild and gentle is her sway,
She scatters with a liberal hand
Choice blessings round us every day.

NOVEMBER (); ALL THE REST HAVE

Now sombre clouds o'erspread the skies,
And cast a gloom o'er hill and lea,
Cold is the wind, bleak storms arise,
And tune their mournful minstrelsy.

THIRTY-ONE (),(),(),

How fierce the wintry tempests howl,
How cheerless is the naked grove,
The skies assume an angry scowl,
And lakes and steamlets cease to move.

The dreary winter months are gone,
And Sol prolongs the hours of day,
But yet no music hails the morn,
No verdure clothes the leafless spring.

The blooming beauties of the spring
With balmy odors fill the air,
And birds with cheerful music sing,
To drive away corroding care.

(),(),(),(),

How grateful is the cooling shade
To those who toil or roam the plain,
When Sol in glowing robes arrayed,
Resumes o'er all his sultry reign.

Now leave the scenes of pampered wealth,
Nor breathe the city's noxious air,
And seek for vigor and for health
In verdant fields and woodlands fair.

Though blooming verdure smiles no more,
And dreary is the landscape round,
Yet autumn's rich and bounteous store
Cause joy and gladness to abound.

Another year its course has run,
And all its scenes forever fled,
How soon will mortal life be done -
And we all numbered with the dead!

EXCEPTING FEBRUARY ALONE (),

Yet time so rapidly moves on,
That snowy fields and wintry skies
Will like a phantom soon be gone,
And other scenes before us rise.

WHICH HATH BUT TWENTY-EIGHT, IN FINE,

TILL LEAP YEAR GIVES IT TWENTY-NINE.

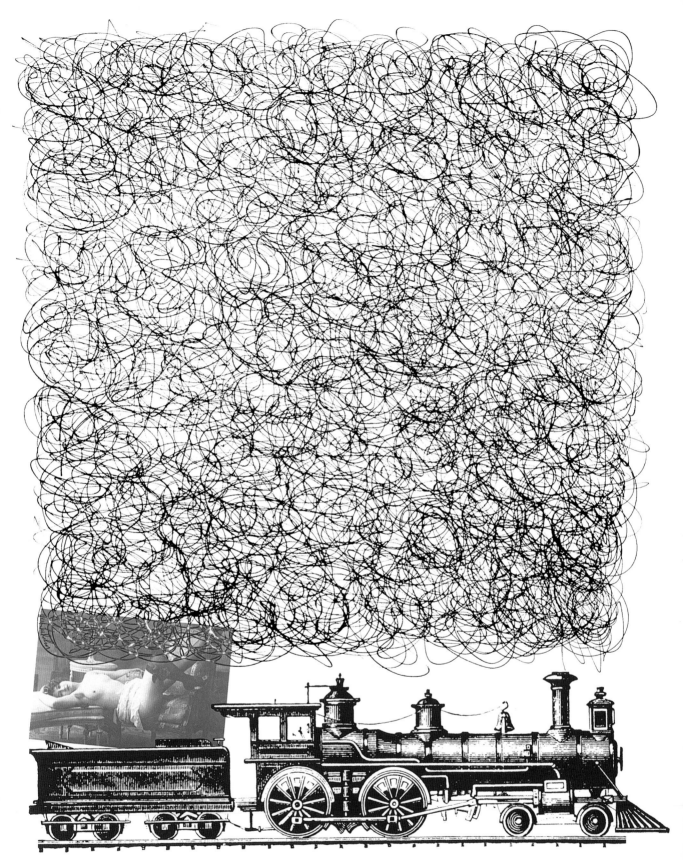

Form Ever Follows Function

Herb and Lou: A Lifelong Bond ハーブとルウの絆

Marion Muller マリオン・マラー

In the advertising and graphics world their names were constantly linked. They were invited often to be joint lecturers, joint judges, joint teachers at seminars. Early in their careers, they talked of collaborating in a studio of their own. And though they once reached the point of discussing whose name should come first on their company letterhead, the logo was never designed, the partnership never happened. As Dorfsman's career flourished at CBS, as Director of Advertising and Design, he found it harder and harder to break away. Lubalin did join in partnerships with others, concentrating more on pure design than advertising. Nevertheless, for 46 years their personal and professional lives were totally entwined.

The friendship started in 1935 at Cooper Union. Scholastically they leaned in different directions—Dorfsman toward 3-dimensional design, Lubalin toward advertising graphics. But in their extra-curricular activities, they were of one mind. They teamed up on dates and on trips to Harlem for jazz concerts. Soon after graduation they married their Cooper Union sweethearts. They chose the same wedding day, honeymooned at the same hotel and, for a while, shared an apartment to save on rent. Forever after they were inseparable, though in their DNA, their personalities and approach to work, they were as different as men could be.

Dorfsman is tall, energetic, expansive. He hugs, he scolds, he teases, he jokes easily and makes his thoughts and feelings clear to everyone. Lubalin was a small man; reticent, more comfortable

広告・グラフィック界でルバリンとドーフスマンの名はいつも一緒に括られていた。2人で講演や審査、セミナーの講師を頼まれることが多く、駆け出しの頃には共同事務所の設立話も持ちあがっている。レターヘッドではどちらの名前を先にするかとまで話し合いながらも、結局ロゴは完成せず、この話が実現されることはなかった。ドーフスマンはCBSの広告・デザインのディレクターとして成功し、そこから抜け出せない状況になった。一方ルバリンは広告よりも純粋なデザインに専念し、他の人と組んで仕事をした。しかしながら、2人の間には公私を通じた46年の深い絆があった。

2人の友情は1935年クーパー・ユニオンで芽生えた。ドーフスマンは立体デザイン、ルバリンは広告グラフィックと別のものを学んでいたが、学校の外では気持ちをひとつにした。連れ立ってデートをしたり、ハーレムのジャズコンサートに通ったりしたのだ。卒業後まもなく彼らはクーパー・ユニオンの学友と結婚した。婚礼には同じ日を選び、新婚旅行のホテルも同じ。しばらくの間節約するためにと、一緒にアパートを借りて部屋を分けたりもした。DNAも性格も仕事の仕方も極めて異なる2人だが、それからもずっと離れることがなかった。

ドーフスマンは背が高く、活動的で開放的だ。人をすぐ抱きしめたり、叱ったり、からかったり、冗談を言ったり。自分の考えや感情をはっきり見せる。ルバリンは背が低く無口で、人と差し向いで話すより大勢の人の前で話す方が好きだった。ルバリンは口数は少なかったが、鉛筆を持つとすごい勢いだった。反対に

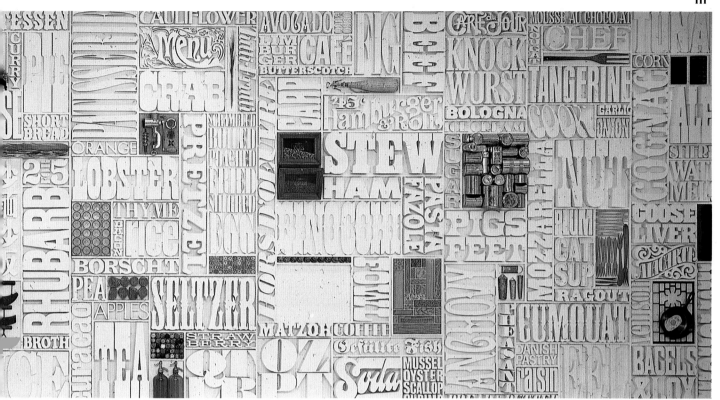

Three-dimensional wall for CBS cafeteria CBSカフェテリアの壁面 1966

lecturing to a crowd than speaking personally, face-to-face. Lubalin was frugal with words, but prodigious with a pencil. Dorfsman, by contrast, works slowly. He examines all angles of a problem before he sets pencil to paper.

In the prime of their careers, Lubalin and Dorfsman became noticeably absorbed with typography as a design element. To them it was not just an afterthought, but a major player. They began to use type pictorially, expressively, for color, for texture, for the sheer beauty of the abstract forms.

Their mutual pleasure and artistry with type were demonstrated in the 40-foot wall (pictured above) created for the CBS cafeteria. Dorfsman conceived of treating the space like an enlarged printers' job case, with a lock-up of words and objects related to food. He designed the first 8-foot section and commissioned Lubalin to design the remaining seven panels in a variety of type faces, sizes, weights and depths. The wall, installed in 1966, was a triumphant Dorfsman-Lubalin collaboration.

When Dorfsman, now retired from CBS, heard recently that the wall was dismantled and about to be trashed, he immediately made plans to salvage it. It will be refurbished and installed in a permanent home at Cooper Union or the new Museum of Advertising currently being planned. Dorfsman's resurrection of the wall is a testament to his intolerance of waste and his respect for fine design. More than that, it will be a monument to the lifelong bond between the men, which still exists for Dorfsman a dozen years after Lubalin's death.

ドーフスマンの仕事はゆっくりだ。紙に鉛筆を走らせる前に、あらゆる角度から問題を検討する。

　全盛期のルバリンとドーフスマンは、デザインエレメントとしてのタイポグラフィに傾倒した。2人にとって、タイポグラフィは後から足すようなものではなく主役だった。文字に色彩やテクスチャーを持たせ、またその抽象的な形の美を見せながら、絵画的、表現的に使い始めた。文字を使った2人の遊びと芸術の結晶が、約12メートルに及ぶCBSのカフェテリア(上)の壁面である。ドーフスマンは食べ物に関係のある言葉やオブジェを入れた、活字ケースを拡大したような空間を思いついた。彼は最初の2.4メートルのパネルをデザインし、ルバリンに残り7枚のパネルを書体や級数、重さ、深さに変化をつけてデザインしてくれるよう依頼した。壁は1966年に設置され、2人の共同制作は成功を収めた。

　ドーフスマンは既にCBSを辞めているが、最近壁が撤去されて捨てられそうだということを聞いて、すぐにその救済計画を立てた。壁は改装され、クーパー・ユニオンか現在計画されている新しい広告美術館に永久保存される予定である。ドーフスマンが壁を復元しようとするのは、無駄に我慢ができない、優れたデザインを大切にしたいという気持からだろう。それだけでなく、この壁はルバリンの死後12年経過してもなお残る、2人の生涯にわたる絆の記念碑となるのであろう。

HERB LUBALIN & **LOU DORFSMAN** ハーブ・ルバリン&*ルウ・ドーフスマン*

Steven Heller スティーブン・ヘラー

After studying Lou Dorfsman's collected print advertisements for CBS produced during the 1960s and 70s, one realizes that ads of this kind are not done anymore. Sure, there is some very clever advertising created today, particularly commercials for TV. But the era of superb, conceptual print advertising in which typography was not simply an afterthought but the basis on which ideas were constructed, is long gone. Dorfsman, who has been retired from CBS for almost a decade, was a master among masters. The 1960s was a period when great advertising typographers were in abundance. This was when advertisements didn't need sex to sell, but rather a catchy phrase or word set in a boldly elegant typeface would suffice.

There is nothing stylish about Dorfsman's design—nothing quaint that would make it a nostalgic preserve—yet everything he has touched reveals an unmistakable style. Dorfsman is fundamentally a classicist but he does not reprise old-fashioned styles. His CBS work was underscored by elegant, classical types, spaced and leaded to perfection, and composed on the page to maximize the impact of white space. His work was modern without conceit. He orchestrated graphics, photographs and illustrations to present what in another designer's hands might well have been dry and pedantic. Given the hardsell genre of institutional advertising, Dorfsman's unique brand of concrete poetics provided the edge that engaged and provoked. His ads did not only look good, they were sublimely witty manifestos.

Among the ads that still resonate—indeed they could be reprised today without changes—is "Ha, Ha, Ha: He laughs best who laughs last." So simple, so eyecatching: the word "Ha" grows larger according to the ratings response to the three television networks' comedy shows, with the largest representing CBS. Without the benefit of a hardsell slogan or sensational image, Dorfsman let type do all the visual persuading. For "Worth Repeating, CBS News" Dorfsman employed bold, disproportionately large quote marks sitting majestically upon a pedestal of selling copy. In harnessing the power of punctuation, these curiously abstract marks have greater shouting range than any single line of type or picture. "Dominate," a series of four ads used to sell potential advertisers on the fact that CBS enjoyed dominance in the ratings, is a classic example of how type talks. Again, without the benefit of an image, Dorfsman used four words—"Captivate!" "Elucidate!", "Fascinate!" and "Exhilarate!"—each set in a different face with an exclamation point dotted with the CBS eye. The copy below suggests the range of CBS's programs in a market it totally controlled.

These and countless other ads did more than remind, inform and persuade clients; they increased the recognition of CBS by giving it a uniform identity. If not for Dorfsman CBS might have had its eye, but with him it had an intelligence. Dorfsman's advertising and promotion for CBS is a monument to how intelligent propaganda can enhance a superb product. It also reveals how, given the right chemistry, an art director and a client can distill the perfect essence.

Few corporations today even have their own in-house advertising and promotion departments; therefore few get the intense commitment that Dorfsman brought to CBS. His work represents an era of excellence. Too bad that era is past.

1960年代から70年代にかけて作られたルウ・ドーフスマンのCBSの広告を見ると、この手のものがなくなってしまったことに気づく。今でも、特にテレビには面白い広告がある。しかし、タイポグラフィが後から付け加えられたのではなくアイディアの基礎にあった、コンセプト重視の優れた新聞雑誌広告が作られた時代は去ってしまった。ドーフスマンがCBSを辞めて10年近く経つが、彼は名人中の名人だった。60年代は広告界に多くの偉大なタイポグラファーがいた時代である。当時の広告はセックスを売り物にする必要などなく、心を引くキャッチフレーズやコピーが、大胆に優雅な文字で組まれていればよかった。

ドーフスマンのデザインには、郷愁を呼ぶ古風なスタイルというような特定の作風はないが、彼の手にかかったものには全て彼のものと分かる何かがある。彼は基本的に古典主義者だが、時代遅れのものを蘇らせようとはしない。CBSの仕事は完璧な詰めの優美で古典的な文字、そして余白を最大限に生かしたレイアウトが特徴だった。奇抜ではないがモダンであった。グラフィックと写真、イラストレーションを組み合わせ、ともすれば無味乾燥で物知り顔になりがちのものを上手に仕上げている。売り込みの強い企業広告の分野にあって、ユニークなタイポグラフィの形体詩は人を魅了し刺激する鋭さを持っていた。彼の広告はきれいなだけでなく、機知に富む声明文なのである。

今だ共感を呼ぶ(そのまま使える)広告に「ハッ、ハッ、ハッ。最後(のテレビ局)で笑う人が一番笑う」というのがある。簡潔で目を引くが、「ハッ」という文字が3大テレビネットワークそれぞれのコメディー番組の視聴率に合わせて次第に大きくなり、最大のCBSで終っている。売り込み文句や意表をつく絵を使わず、ドーフスマンは文字に視覚的なもの全てを語らせた。「ぜひ伝えたい、CBSニュース」ではコピーを堂々と囲む太くて異様に大きい引用符を配した。抽象的な符号は1行のコピーや1枚の写真よりずっと説得力を持つのである。「優位」はCBSが視聴率で優位に立つ事実を元に、潜在的広告主に向けられた4点シリーズ広告だが、文字の雄弁さを証明した傑作である。彼はここでも絵の助けを借りず、「心を奪う!」、「解明する!」、「魅惑する!」、「興奮させる!」と4つの言葉を使った。おのおの別の書体を使いながら、感嘆符の点はみなCBSの「目」のシンボルになっている。コピーはCBSの番組の幅広さ、マーケットを独占しているという事実を示す。

他にも数えられないほどある彼の広告は、クライアントに気づかせる、知らせる、促すというだけでなく、統一的なイメージでCBSの認知度を高めた。ドーフスマンがいなくても「目」のシンボルはあったかもしれないが、彼がいたからこそCBSは知性を持ったのだ。彼が制作したCBSの広告とプロモーションは、知的な宣伝活動がいかに優れた商品をより良くしたかという典型である。またアートディレクターとクライアントの息が合えば、いかにいいものが生まれるかを示している。

今日の企業はほとんど自社の広告販促部門を持たず、CBSに対するドーフスマンのような熱心なかかわり合いもまず目にすることがない。彼の作品は優れたものを求める時代の代表である。その時代が過去のものとなってしまったのは全く残念なことである。

IGOR STRAVINSKY'S
"NOAH AND THE FLOOD"
CHOREOGRAPHED BY
GEORGE BALANCHINE

*An original dance drama based on the familiar Biblical theme, with Laurence Harvey, Sebastian Cabot,
Jacques d'Amboise, and Elsa Lanchester; performed by the New York City Ballet, and produced by Sextant Inc.
A Breck Golden Showcase presentation. Commissioned by the CBS Television Network.*

WORLD PREMIERE TONIGHT 9:00 TO 10:00 CBS●2

1 Newspaper ad for TV program テレビ番組の新聞広告 1962

THE GERSHWIN YEARS

The CBS Television Network presents a 90-minute musical extravaganza with Richard Rodgers as host—starring Maurice Chevalier, Florence Henderson, Ron Husmann, Julie London, Frank Sinatra and Ethel Merman...Produced by Leland Hayward.

8:00 TO 9:30 TONIGHT ON CBS ● CHANNEL 2

A Dickens Chronicle

No single individual conjures up the world of 19th Century England as vividly as Charles Dickens—a world of cosy inns and roaring fires, of grinding poverty and social injustice.

Tonight at 7:30 EST, CBS News brings this world to life in a compelling broadcast in which episodes from the novelist's tormented personal life are presented in dramatic counterpoint to some of the celebrated creations of his soaring imagination.

Dominating the screen is the memorable figure of Mr. Pickwick's famous manservant—Sam Weller—who alternates between presenting fellow characters from the various novels and providing the biographical background to scenes from Dickens' family life. You are happily bewildered by the plump and garrulous Mrs. Nickleby expounding her fuzzy notions. You are shocked by the browbeating schoolmaster, Wackford Squeers. You are touched by the foolish optimism of Mr. Micawber: "until something turns up I have nothing to bestow but advice." You are delighted by the innocence and warmth of Mr. Pickwick himself as Sam Weller introduces him to Weller, Sr., "the old 'un" over a glass of brandy.

And in between this colorful parade of characters you enter the Dickens household at various stages—in his childhood as the son of a father imprisoned for debt; in the days of his courtship as a young, romantic writer; and in the crowning years of his success as one of the greatest literary figures the world has produced. As he himself wrote: "My whole nature was so penetrated by the grief and humiliation of such considerations (his father's imprisonment) that even now, famous and caressed and happy, I often forget in my dreams that I have a dear wife and children…even that I am a man…and wander desolately back to that time of my life."

Performed by a distinguished cast starring Clive Revill as Sam Weller; Robert Stephens as Dickens; Rosemary Harris as his wife, Kate; and Douglas Campbell as Mr. Micawber, tonight's broadcast offers a unique viewing experience for the entire family.

The influence of great men on their times is no less of a reality than the latest news report of a fire, an act of Congress, or a labor dispute. In tonight's broadcast CBS News reaches into the realities of a past century to illuminate its customs, manners and conditions, just as it reaches into today's international realities and tomorrow's technological realities to present an interview with Chancellor Adenauer, a military expedition in Southeast Asia, a space launching from Cape Canaveral. To a resourceful and enterprising news organization all reality is its province.

CBS NEWS

RUSSIANS: SELF IMPRESSIONS

On the principle that the life of a nation is reflected in its literature, the Public Affairs Department of CBS News offers a revealing insight into the character of the Russian people tonight at 7:30 EST in a special full hour broadcast based on the works of five famous Russian authors.

As host on the program "Russians: Self-Impressions," Prof. Ernest J. Simmons, noted authority on Russian literature, presents a social and historical commentary on the dramatic presentations. "In this program," he declares, "we seek an insight into the often enigmatic character of the Russian…. To gain that insight into the Russian as he is, we must try to understand the Russian as he was … to know something of the world he grew out of and revolted against."

This world is sharply revealed in scenes from Gogol's classic story "The Overcoat" and Chekhov's drama "The Cherry Orchard." They disclose the poverty and decadence of much of Russian life in the 19th century; while a pervading sense of injustice and futility is reflected in other vignettes from Dostoevsky's "The Brothers Karamazov" and Turgenev's "Fathers and Sons." In introducing the concluding scene from Pasternak's "Dr. Zhivago," Professor Simmons declares—"As with us all, when the social structure crumbles, the only order in the world is to be found in the love one human being can have for another."

A brilliant cast starring Jo Van Fleet, Kim Hunter, Sam Wanamaker, George Voskovec and Joseph Buloff portray the principal characters in the five dramatic sketches.

In employing the literature of the past to illuminate the present, CBS News offers still another example of its many-faceted effort to explore all possible resources that can give meaning to our times. Other instances of this same effort can be seen in the clarification of social and economic issues on CBS REPORTS; in the pages of recent history turned back on THE TWENTIETH CENTURY; in the march of events broadcast each week on EYEWITNESS; and, in fact, in the regularly scheduled daily news reports. To watch them is to gain deeper understanding of the world we live in.

CBS TELEVISION NETWORK

NEXT TUESDAY FOR AN HOUR
(NEXT SEASON-EVERY WEEK!)

Tuesday, March 19, 8:30-9:30 pm EST—JUDY GARLAND AND HER GUESTS, PHIL SILVERS AND ROBERT GOULET—on the CBS Television Network ⊙

5 Newspaper ad for TV program テレビ番組の新聞広告 1963

THE NEW YORK TIMES, FRIDAY, JANUARY 26, 1962

THE ROCKET'S RED GLARE...

Early tomorrow morning – if all goes well – the eyes of a nation, and its hopes and prayers, will be focused on the first attempt of an American to orbit the earth.

As the rocket propelling Lt. Col. John H. Glenn, Jr., soars into space, the magic of television will enable millions of his fellow Americans to share in one of the great moments of their history.

Starting at 7:00 a.m., the CBS Television Network will stand ready to transmit continuous pooled reports of Colonel Glenn's three-orbit flight starting with the advance preparations for the lift-off to his recovery some six to eight hours later in the waters off the Bahamas.

REPORT ON RECOVERY

The CBS Television Network will interrupt its program schedule to present the video-tape report of Colonel Glenn's recovery the moment it becomes available. Should the flight be postponed, the network will, of course, broadcast the event whenever it is scheduled.

For its own special coverage and supplementing the pooled reports of the event, CBS News has assembled the largest complement of reporters, technical personnel, and facilities ever concentrated on a single news event with the exception of the national conventions and elections. Stationed at the CBS News control center adjacent to the launching site at Cape Canaveral, CBS News "anchor man" Walter Cronkite, assisted by Charles von Fremd and Richard Bate, will provide a running commentary at the missile area. The event will also be broadcast by the CBS Radio Network with CBS News correspondent Dallas Townsend as "anchor man" and Arthur Godfrey providing commentary.

To picture the course of the flight, a model of the capsule will be moved by magnets on a flat projection map showing the astronaut's location at any given moment. In addition, two animated globes will also reveal the orbital course.

HOW TO FLY A CAPSULE

CBS News will also present a striking demonstration of how to "fly" a capsule in a special 20-minute filmed report showing an engineer manipulating the controls of a capsule identical to the space craft carrying Colonel Glenn on his journey.

From London, Paris, and Moscow CBS News correspondents will report foreign reactions to the flight; while in Washington CBS News reporters Roger Mudd and Neil Strawser will describe Congressional reactions and the United States Information Agency's broadcasts throughout the world. From New York CBS News Moscow correspondent Marvin Kalb and UN correspondent Richard C. Hottelet will describe the Soviet man-in-space program and contrast the relative secrecy of the Russian experience with the full publicity surrounding the American effort.

FAMILY REACTIONS

In New Concord, Ohio, Colonel Glenn's home town, CBS News correspondents Harry Reasoner and Hughes Rudd will interview the astronaut's parents and report the mass gathering of the town's 2100 citizens at Muskingum College to watch the broadcast. In Arlington, Virginia, CBS News correspondent Nancy Hanschman will report the reactions of Mrs. Glenn, her children, and her parents at their home.

For the benefit of the thousands of daily commuters and other travelers in Grand Central Station, a giant screen will report the flight, as CBS News correspondent Doug Edwards moves through the crowds to pick up the reactions of the public.

Finally, if all goes according to schedule, CBS News will present a special report tomorrow night at 7:30 p.m. reviewing the highlights of the day's events and including the press conference with top NASA officials following the completion of the flight.

Tomorrow will be a day to remember as television once again demonstrates its unique power to enlarge and deepen the range of human experience. From the dawn's early light to the twilight's last gleaming, you can see it all.

CBS⊙2

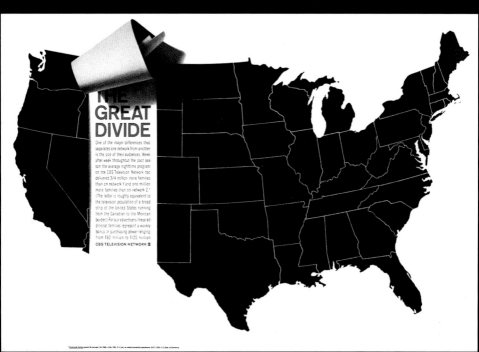

ha ha ha

he laughs best ⊛ who laughs last

Some people started laughing right off the bat when they heard we planned to concentrate on comedy this season. They were sure it wouldn't work. These days they're not laughing so hard—but the nation's viewers are, and so are the sponsors of our comedy programs. The audiences attracted by the average comedy program on the three networks this season tell the story: Network Y—7.3 million homes…Network Z—8.9 million homes…CBS Television Network, 9.5 million homes.* Moreover, in the latest Nielsen report three of our funniest shows are in the Top 10—and two of them are brand new this season.† But the thing that keeps all our advertisers smiling is that the CBS Television Network attracts the biggest average audiences in every category of entertainment, laughs or no laughs.

CBS Television Network

7 Newspaper ad for TV network テレビネットワークの新聞広告 1962

THE GREAT DIVIDE

One of the major differences that separates one network from another is the size of their audiences. Week after week throughout the past season the average nighttime program on the CBS Television Network has delivered 3/4 million more families than on network Y and one million more families than on network Z.* (The latter is roughly equivalent to the television population of a broad strip of the United States running from the Canadian to the Mexican border.) For our advertisers these additional families represent a weekly bonus in purchasing power ranging from $152 million to $200 million.

CBS TELEVISION NETWORK ⊛

8 Newspaper ad for TV network テレビネットワークの新聞広告 1965

Worth | Repeating

"The Columbia Broadcasting System turned in a superb journalistic beat last night, running away with the major honors in reporting President Johnson's election victory. In clarity of presentation the network led all the way…In a medium where time is of the essence the performance of C.B.S. was of landslide proportions. The difference…lay in the C.B.S. sampling process called Vote Profile Analysis …the C.B.S. staff called the outcome in state after state before its rivals." THE NEW YORK TIMES (11/4/64)

"…VPA is now the most modern of election reporting techniques. It enabled CBS to demolish its competition Tuesday night. In 1962, and again in 1964, CBS has proved superior." CHICAGO DAILY NEWS (11/5/64)

"Long before 4:03 a.m., when Walter Cronkite breathed 'good night,' it was apparent that for quick, comprehensible, interesting reporting and projecting of the night's returns, neither NBC nor ABC had matched CBS." NEWSWEEK (11/16/64)

⊛CBS | News

WHITE VS WHITE
WHITE VS BLACK
BLACK VS BLACK
BLACK VS WHITE
WHITE VS YELLOW
YELLOW VS YELLOW
YELLOW VS BROWN
BROWN VS BROWN

WATCH THE WORLDWATCHERS CBS NEWS

10

Nixon watches Kosygin.
Kosygin watches Mao.
Mao watches Ho.
Ho watches Ky
(Who watches Thieu).
Nasser watches Dayan.
Dayan watches DeGaulle.
DeGaulle watches Nixon.
Cronkite watches Everybody.

WATCH
THE WORLDWATCHERS CBS NEWS

11

ABM, NLF, DMZ, SAM,
LEM, HEW, DEW, FCC,
LSD, DNA, HRA, UAR,
HUD, FTC, CIA, AMA,
ABA, OEO, FDA, SDS,
SOS!

WATCH
THE
WORLDWATCHERS
CBS NEWS

Captivate!

Women are watching more daytime television than ever before, and watching more of it on the CBS Television Network than on any other. And with good reason. Day after day they can anticipate exciting new chapter in their favorite daytime dramas—among the longest running programs in television. In fact, back in 1950, this network was the one to introduce the whole idea of daytime television, opening up to housewives a wonderful world of entertainment and information throughout the day: A world that could captivate them with inventive games. A world where they could watch CBS News' distinguished correspondents elucidate the crucial issues of our time. A world in which a Captain Kangaroo could fascinate not only children but mothers as well. In short, a world of daytime programming that would captivate the biggest audiences in network television, as it has for the past three consecutive years. There's no question about it: when it comes to having a way with women, advertisers can always depend on the CBS Television Network to **Dominate**

13

ELUCIDATE!

Deadlock on disarmament, blockade in Berlin, conflict in the Congo, tornado in Texas—wherever and whenever it happens, the nation's viewers will know and understand it better when exposed to the crisp reporting and clarifying insights of CBS News' distinguished staff of correspondents and cameramen stationed throughout the world. Measured by whatever yardstick you may choose—enterprise, experience, reliability or acclaim, they add up to what

The New York Times has called "the ablest news staff in broadcasting"—a reputation for responsibility that goes back over a quarter of a century to the days when CBS News pioneered such broadcasting techniques as the foreign news round-up and the documentary in depth. These qualities were never in more demand than they are today, as the events and issues of our time grow increasingly urgent and complex. It is these qualities that continue to insure the respect and confidence of the public in CBS News—and offer still further evidence that in the coming season the program schedule of the CBS Television Network will continue to **DOMINATE**

14

FASCINATE!

What may well turn out to be a landmark in television drama will take place on Sunday night, October 29, on the CBS Television Network. Sir Laurence Olivier and Julie Harris, supported by one of the finest casts ever assembled, will appear in a magnificent two-hour production of "The Power and the Glory." They are part of the unprecedented array of performers, producers, directors and playwrights whose talents will be on display during the coming weeks. In the course of this notable dramatic season the network will present six original Westinghouse specials (sample: "The Dispossessed" with Ralph Bellamy, Dina

Merrill, and Earl Holliman), four adaptations of famous classics on The Golden Showcase (sample: "The Picture of Dorian Grey" by Oscar Wilde); and Leland Hayward's "The Good Years" a brilliant evocation of the century's early years. And beyond these glittering highlights viewers will be enthralled week in and week out by The U. S. Steel Hour, Armstrong Circle Theatre, The Twilight Zone, The Defenders and G. E. Theater. A kaleidoscopic world of drama unmatched in television and offering still further evidence that **DOMINATE** the CBS Television Network has the flair, balance and quality to

15

E HILARATE!

This Fall, the CBS Television Network will again chalk up the biggest attendance record in football. The same go-go-go spirit that first brought professional football home to a nationwide audience (the late National Football League Commissioner Bert Bell attributed the game's phenomenal rise to this network's pioneering coverage) is also responsible for many other CBS Television Network sports firsts. First to give the nation a front row seat at international competitions through exclusive coverage of the 1960 Winter and Summer Olympics. First to use video tape in sports, making it possible to rerun thoroughbred races, crucial golf rounds and scoring football plays as soon as

they are over. First to televise the whole incredible range of sporting events from rugby to auto racing, from sky diving to figure skating—through the introduction of the weekly Sports Spectacular series. And throughout the year, this network continues to bring a hundred million television fans such major events of every season as the college bowl games, the Triple Crown, the UN Handicap, the PGA and Masters golf tournaments, and baseball's Major League Games of the Week. Sports play an exhilarating, exciting part in the powerful CBS Television Network **DOMINATE** line-up, which again this season has the balance, depth and quality to

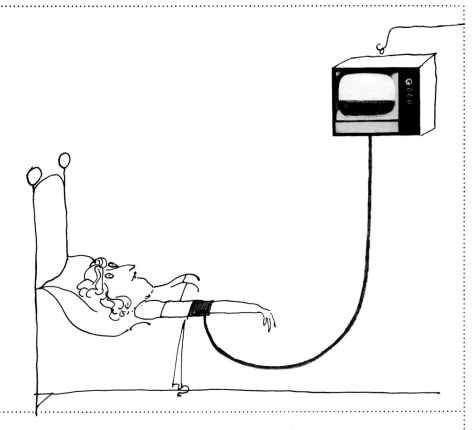

Some women can't live without it.
Indeed, our daytime line-up is such
a vital part of their lives that
the 9 most popular programs are
all ours. Of our 16 daytime programs,
12 are in the Top 15. The ladies
have taken us to their hearts.
CBS Television Network ◉

17 Newspaper and magazine ad for TV network テレビネットワークの新聞・雑誌広告 1969

18 Title for TV program テレビ番組のタイトル 1973

A Glossary of Television Terms

Some illustrations of recent additions to our lexicon as striking as the changes in our nation's habits: last year the average American television family spent more time viewing than ever before – 5 hours and 17 minutes a day.

All Out. When a picture previously superimposed on another is removed from the original picture.

Eye Cam'er-a. A camera specially designed to simulate the movement of the eyes on a reading surface.

Juic'er. Any television electrician who is especially trained and equipped to work with heavy power lines.

Nut. As applied to television, the complete cost of producing a program. Also called, "the whole nut."

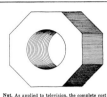

Town Cri'er. A slang expression which refers to a vocalist who is noted for exceptional strength of voice.

Au'di-o. That portion of a television transmission pertaining to sound as opposed to the picture (video).

Fish Bowl. An observation booth, sometimes overlooking the studio, which contains television monitors.

Jump. The elimination of a previously planned scene from a film, which requires the film to be resplied.

One Shot. (a) Single show as opposed to series. (b) One installment script. (c) Subject which fills screen.

Trap. An opening in the stage floor which permits the performers to make their entrances and exits.

Ba'by Spot'light. The smallest of the incandescent spotlights which utilizes 100-watt or 150-watt bulbs.

Flood. A light which projects a broad, well-diffused beam on a set, encompassing all subjects in a scene.

Key'light. The principal source of directional illumination which falls upon a given object, area or scene.

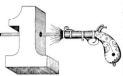

Out'line. The synopsis or initial written account of a proposed television program. Also called scenario.

Ve-ne'tian Blind. A video tape displacement of lines in a band, causing a sawtooth vertical picture edge.

Bull'frog. The slang expression for a television performer with an exceptionally deep, resonant voice.

Gal'lows. An open frame which supports drapes and allows the cameras and equipment to pass through.

Kill. To order the elimination of any production element, including scene, set, action or the entire show.

Pan. To follow the action of any scene to the left or to the right by the gradual swinging of the camera.

View'er. (a) Person watching a television program. (b) Machine used to study film for editing purposes.

Cam'er-a Hog. A performer who monopolizes camera action to the exclusion of other persons in a scene.

Ground Cloth. A large section of waterproof canvas used as a protective or decorative cover for the stage.

Lick. An ad-libbed musical phrase which does not appear in the score. An ad lib in jazz is a "hot lick."

Per'i-scope. A special arrangement of mirrors which permits making camera shots not normally possible.

Wings. Entrance and storage area immediately offstage concealed from the camera or studio audience.

Core. The plastic or metal center section upon which film is often wound for storage or shipping purposes.

Hand Props. Movable materials of any description which are used or carried on stage by a performer.

Lock'jaw. (a) A performer who delivers lines without expression. (b) A vocalist who lacks inspiration.

Ride it. An instruction to the orchestra members on a television program to improvise or ad lib the score.

Woof. The word sometimes spoken into a microphone to check amplitude or to synchronize timing.

Dis-tor'tion. A picture change produced deliberately for special effect, or caused by equipment failure.

Hiss. A disturbing sound appearing at random in the audio frequency range of a television broadcast.

Me-chan'i-cal An-i-ma'tion. Drawings of inanimate objects given movement through a device called a rig.

Roll. A television picture which flips up and down due to improper synchronization or power source.

Zoom. Effect created by variable focus lens to make the subject appear to move to or from the camera.

Drop. Scenery which is suspended from metal framework or grid near the studio roof and is not framed.

Ink'er. Artist who traces the animator's drawings on celluloid sections which are later photographed.

Min'i-a-ture. Models of large objects (houses, automobiles, props) which appear as normal on camera.

Slide. A transparent frame of film which is mounted between two pieces of glass for use in a projector.

Lead'er-ship. The quality invariably associated with the CBS Television Network. e.g. 1. Biggest average daytime audiences for six consecutive years. 2. Biggest average nighttime audiences for nine years. 3. Specifically, this season* CBS delivers one million more homes, both day and night, than the second network; two million more than the third. 4. Since 1954, this Network has been the world's largest single advertising medium. CBS Television Network⊙

Ex-po'sure. To subject photographic film to the light in order to produce a hidden image on the emulsion.

In-te'ri-or Sounds. The sounds of an object, such as a train, as they would be heard from within the object.

Net. An abbreviation for network or multiple television stations linked by coaxial cables or microwaves.

Slow Mo'tion. To photograph at faster than normal rate so that the projected action will appear slower.

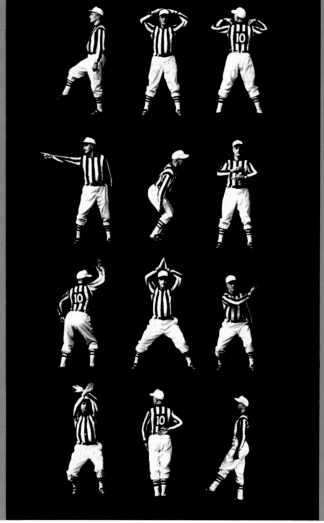

20 Shipping container for book about football フットボール写真集のケース 1969

23 Logotype for EVR ビデオシステムのロゴタイプ 1981

22 Logotype for art dealers association 美術商協会のロゴタイプ 1979

21 Logotype for boys clothing manufacturer 男児服メーカーのロゴタイプ 1973

24 Logotype for CBS music division CBS音楽部門のロゴタイプ 1981

25 Logotype for cable TV network ケーブルテレビのロゴタイプ 1982

26 Logotypes for TV election coverage 大統領選挙報道用ロゴタイプ 1968-76

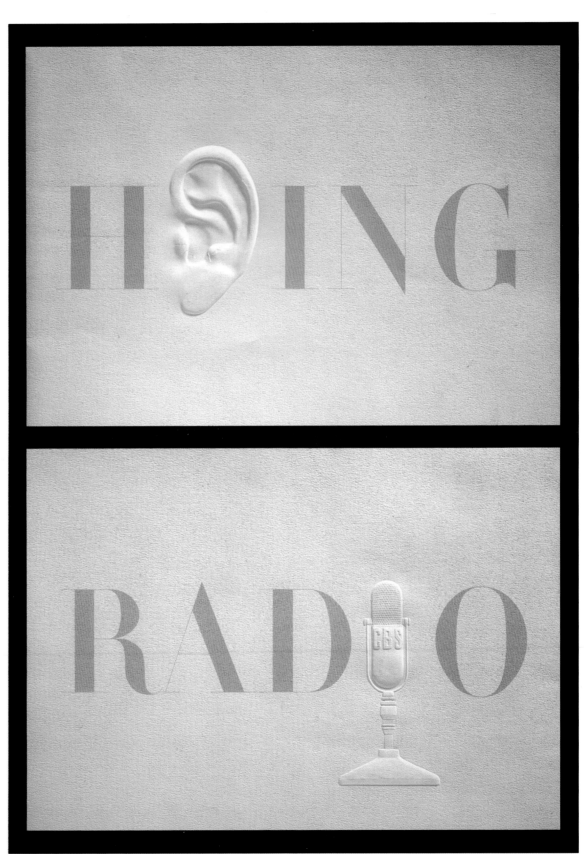

27 Front and back covers for radio station brochure ラジオ局のパンフレット表紙

WIZARD OF WOR

Burwors, Garwors, Thorwors, Worluk and Wizard await you in the Dreaded Dungeons

WIZARD OF WOR

For use with the Atari® Video Computer Systems™

CBS VIDEO GAMES

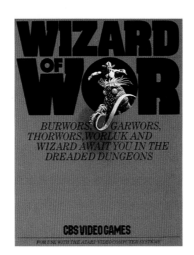

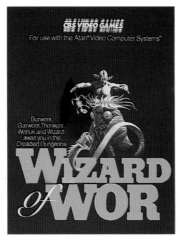

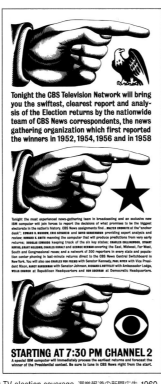

29 Newspaper ad for TV election coverage 選挙報道の新聞広告 1960

30 Annual report cover 年次報告書の表紙 1970

31 Annual report cover 年次報告書の表紙 1976

Consider the egg. Dansk® did. One of nature's most satisfying and useful forms, it signifies the beginning of things. The beginning of Dansk things was 10 years ago, when this first Fjord spoon was hand-forged. Its success egged us on to create a number of other fine objects. Tawny teakwood bowls. A candlestick crowned with twelve thin tapers. Dusky Flamestone cups. An enamelled casserole as bright as a sunflower. And linens with rainbows in their warp and woof. Today there are 493 Dansk designs. Every

one made for daily use. And not an everyday piece in the lot. They all appear in a new 96-page book, a book with the good form to be absolutely free. Write Dansk Designs Ltd, Dept. O, Mount Kisco, N.Y.

32-34 Magazine ads for tableware manufacturer 食器メーカーの雑誌広告 1962

Black is beautiful
White is beautiful

Købenstyle is beautiful. And has been for years—in red, yellow and blue. Now we introduce two new colors —black, and white. The only two colors as basic as the original three. Notice how the natural color of food is vividly enhanced against black and white. Potatoes, tomatoes, carrots, beef, (even boeuf), seem to be more tempting in these pots. If you like our black and white, just wait until you see our full color brochure of 596 tabletop classics. Send 10¢ to Dansk Designs Ltd., Dept. BW, Mt. Kisco, N.Y. 10549. **DANSK DESIGNS LTD.**

33 1982

SUPER BOWL

Only 350 fortunate people will get to our Super Bowl this year. Each will pay $250...a modest price for this true piece of art from famed designer Jens Quistgaard. His teak bowl is a full 17 inches across and a stately 53 inches around the waist. It will grace a sideboard and splendidly present a salad for a festive buffet elegantly serving six or sixteen.

We'd like to make more than 350 Super Bowls, but there isn't enough flawless aged teak to be found... nor are there enough master craftsmen schooled in the great Dansk tradition of woodworking. This scarcity suggests the heirloom value of each magnificent bowl. So although only 350 people can own one, thousands will enjoy it.

DANSK
INTERNATIONAL DESIGNS

34 1987

The end
of the
plain white
tablecloth.

You'll still see a few around. In old-timey hotels. Grandma's house. But, really, white has had it. Behind this shift to color is a finicky Finnish fabric designer named Ritva Puotila. She designed this collection just for us.

How do you design a solid-color fabric? By not making it solid. Ours are woven from two colors of yarn. (Pistachio, for instance, is gold and green.) You can't get rich, glowing colors like these by dipping white cloth in a dye-vat.

Curiously enough, only Dansk™ makes yarn-dyed napkins and tablecloths like these.

We call them "Finnish Accent." You can mix them or match them in any combination you choose. Because they're designed that way.

There are 493 other designs for the well-dressed table in our 96 page catalog. For your copy send 25¢ to Dansk Designs Ltd., Dept. E, Mt. Kisco, New York 10549. And don't throw out your white tablecloths. They may be back in style some day.

Dansk Designs Ltd.

35 1971

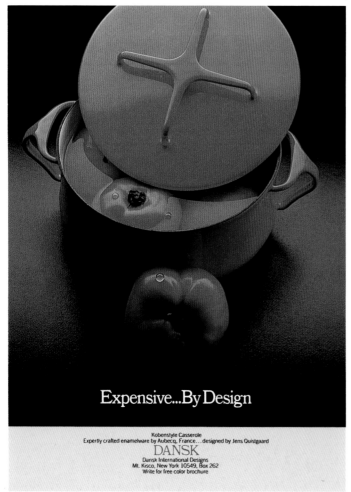

Expensive...By Design

Kobenstyle Casserole
Expertly crafted enamelware by Aubecq, France... designed by Jens Quistgaard
DANSK
Dansk International Designs
Mt. Kisco, New York 10549, Box 262
Write for free color brochure

36 1972

Expensive...By Design

Teak Bread Board
Hand assembled endwood... designed by Jens Quistgaard
DANSK
Dansk International Designs
Mt. Kisco, New York 10549, Box 721
Write for free color brochure

37 1972

FRANSK.

Introducing the Dansk® collection of fine French crystal. Dansk in France? Why not? When Jens Quistgaard designed this group for us, he knew we would find the finest craftsmen to make the pieces, wherever the search took us. It took us, of course, to France, where appreciation of stemware is legendary. (Surely, French-men have spent more time gazing thoughtfully into wineglasses than any other people.) Our crystal collection consists of five patterns, each in three sizes; each French in body but Dansk in spirit. This is Dansk's entry into crystal making. Now we can truthfully say that we make everything for the tabletop, from the cloth to the candle-flame. If you know us for our wood, china, silver, steel, iron, enamel and so on, you know the quality we bring to our stemware. If you don't know us, know us. Send 25¢ for our new catalog of 493 wonderful things. Write to Dansk Designs Ltd., Department G, Mt. Kisco, New York 10549.

DANSK DESIGNS LTD.

39　1970

How to be graceful though short and fat.

Who would have thought a candle as high as it is wide could be as poised and pretty as this? Who but Dansk? We pack them six to a box, each on its own vineyard green glass base, in subtle two-color combinations. Put one in front of each place setting. Group them in a glowing ring for a holiday centerpiece. Set them in the dimmer corners of an intimate party room. At only $6.95 the package, you can act as if you had candles to burn.
Choose white and brean, red and orange, or aegean and pine, all with green glass bases, handsomely gift-packed 6 to a box. For our new 96-page catalog show-ing 493 other Dansk 'Top of the Table' items, send 25¢ to Dansk Designs Ltd., Dept. A, Mt. Kisco, New York.

38　1968

Jens Quistgaard gives crystal the heft of a tankard, the grace of a chalice. No wispy stems, no lifted pinkies. Instead, a hand-sized handhold on fac-eted or Doric-columned crystal. This pure lead crystal comes in six Quistgaard patterns, each in three

sizes. It's all part of the new tabletop architecture in our current color brochure. To get 576 more-or-less monumental ideas of this kind send a thin dime to Dansk Designs Ltd., Dept. Z, Mt. Kisco, N.Y. 10549.

DANSK DESIGNS LTD.

Put fine wine on a pedestal. It's good for your skål.

35-40　Magazine ads for tableware manufacturer　食器メーカーの雑誌広告　1972

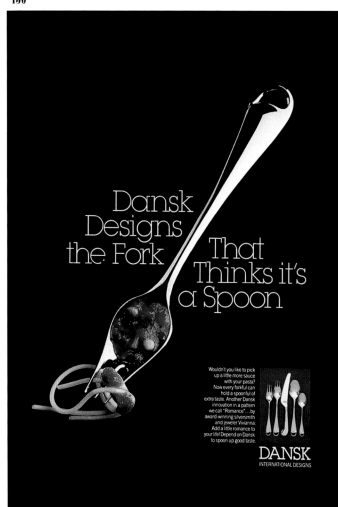

41 1987

42 1983

43 1978

GOOD DESIGN STANDS UP

Dansk puts a new twist on classic flatware. This "Torun" pattern in silverplate (and stainless) created by silversmith and jeweler Vivianna, does more than merely allow the knife to stand on its blade. It also feels extraordinarily easy in the hand. For innovative design ideas, trust Dansk to be on the cutting edge.

DANSK
INTERNATIONAL DESIGNS

NIKLAUS TROXLER ニクラウス・トロクスラー

Catherine Bürer カトリーヌ・ビューラー

Niklaus Troxler acquired his artistic reputation through his jazz concert posters; it is on music that his creative genius was nurtured. To Troxler, music and imagery go hand in hand. His posters represent the result of a dialogue between two elements, vision and sound. Each work is a visual expression of the music which it illustrates; the artist's goal is to show us visually what we can perceive acoustically. Though made with great care and precision, Troxler's jazz posters invariably reveal a spontaneous and improvisational character that mirrors the mood of the music for which they were created. Yet despite the fame and acclaim they have brought him, jazz posters are only one of Troxler's strengths. In fact he creates posters on a wealth of themes, including consumer goods, cultural events, exhibitions and shows.

Troxler developed his unique style—direct, vibrant, expressive—early on. It is a style that is readily recognized in the colors which he employs: colors which are vivid, alive and always pure. They attack us, but not by force, rather attracting our attention with their frank directness. As most of Troxler's posters relate to jazz, his motifs are often similar: saxophones, pianos, hands, bodies in motion, birds, national flags. Such is the alphabet which Troxler uses to express himself. It is his creative genius—and the pleasure which he takes in his artistic games—that enables him to produce infinite variations on themes which are often fundamentally alike.

Stylistically, Troxler does not belong to any one school. His aim is simply to lure the viewer away from his daily routine and offer him an entertaining distraction. It is no surprise to note that Troxler was influenced greatly by Herbert Leupin, an artist whose goal was always to speak to the man in the street, to set up a rapport between poster and passerby. Troxler follows the same path: like Leupin he seeks to charm, to astonish and to provoke.

Tracing back to the 1970s, Troxler's works can be divided into a number of stylistic periods. At various times he has fallen under the influence of surrealism, pop art, a surprising blend of these two (in his 1976 poster for pianist Cecil Taylor), or pure typography (his posters for the McCoy Tyner Sextet in 1980 and for the Thelonious Monk Memorial at MOMA in New York in 1986). In the 1980s he introduced a style even more tense and disjointed, rapid and rhythmic, almost graffiti-like. Then in the 1990s he began adopting a more mechanical view of humanity, using strokes that call to mind the geometry of information signs. But at the same time, being a born experimentalist, he also took to creating new posters of a more pictorial, spontaneous ilk. Through every phase Troxler has been rigidly consistent in one matter: he always insists on creating his posters in his own studio, alone, without outside assistance.

A poster created by Troxler for a one-man show in 1991 perhaps epitomizes the effect which he is ultimately seeking. In it, colored circles bring our focus of attention toward the center, while at the same time they explode outward toward the perimeter, as if wanting to take possession of the surrounding space. The poster is Troxler's portrayal of movement, of vibration, in other words, his portrayal of life itself.

　ニクラウス・トロクスラーは、ジャズコンサートのポスターでその名を知られるようになった。彼のクリエイティブな才能は、音楽によって培われたのである。トロクスラーの中で音楽とイメージは相互に関わりながら進行する。彼のポスターは、視覚と音響という2つの要素の対話から生まれる。作品はそれぞれの音楽を視覚的に表現したものである。つまり聴こえるものを見える形にしようというわけである。とても丁寧に作られているのにもかかわらず、いつものびのびとした即興的なタッチに見え、テーマである音楽の雰囲気をかもしだす。ジャズポスターで名声を得たとはいえ、トロクスラーの魅力はこれだけではない。彼は商品、文化イベント、展覧会と多くのものを題材にポスターを制作している。

　トロクスラーは早くから、率直で活気にあふれた、表情豊かな、独特のスタイルを展開した。それは彼の用いる、鮮やかで生き生きした、混じり気のない色を見ればすぐ分かる。この色彩は力ずくではない、ざっくばらんな魅力で視線を引きつける。ポスターのほとんどがジャズをテーマにしているので、サキソフォーン、ピアノ、手、身振り、鳥、旗といった似たようなモチーフが登場する。それらはトロクスラーが表現するための「アルファベット」なのだ。基本的には同じようなテーマで無限のバリエーションを生み出せるところが彼の才能であり、また彼の創造的な「あそび」の部分でもある。

　トロクスラーの作風はどの流派にも属さない。彼はただ、見る者を単調な日常から解き放ち、楽しさを与えようとしているだけである。いつも道行く人びとに語りかけポスターと彼らの関係を大事にしていたアーティスト、ハーバート・ロイピンの多大な影響を受けたというのも納得がいく。トロクスラーは、人々を魅了し、驚かせ、刺激しようというロイピンと同じ道をたどっているのである。

　1970年代までさかのぼって見ると、彼のスタイルはいくつかの時期に区分することができる。シュールレアリスム、ポップアート、そしてその2つの驚くべき取り合せ（1976年制作のピアニスト、セシル・テイラーのポスター）、純粋なタイポグラフィー（1980年制作マッコイ・タイナー・セクステット、1986年制作セロニアス・モンクを記念したMOMAのポスター）と時期によって様々な影響を受けている。1980年代には緊張感と混乱、スピード感とリズムを持った、ほとんど落書きに近いスタイルを生み出した。1990年代に入ってからは、ピクトグラムの幾何学を連想させる線で、より機械的な目で人間を描くようになった。しかしまた同時に、生まれつきの実験主義者である彼は、より絵画的で自然な表現のポスターも作っている。ただ、どういう場合でも彼はあるひとつのことを固く守っている。いつも自分のスタジオで、独りで、他の人の力を借りずに作るということである。

　1991年の個展のためのポスターが、おそらく彼の追求する効果を集約している。彩られたいくつかの円が、見る者の目を中心に向かわせると同時に、周囲の空間を占めるかのように外に向かって弾けている。そこには動きがあり、振動があり、すなわち生命がある。

A TRIBUTE TO THE MUSIC OF THELONIOUS MONK. Freitag 5. September '86, 20.30 Uhr, Mohren

Jon Hendricks George Adams Bill Hardman Walter Davis jun. Stafford James and Cliff Barbaro

1 "A Tribute to the Music of Thelonious Monk"「セロニアス・モンクの音楽に捧ぐ」1986

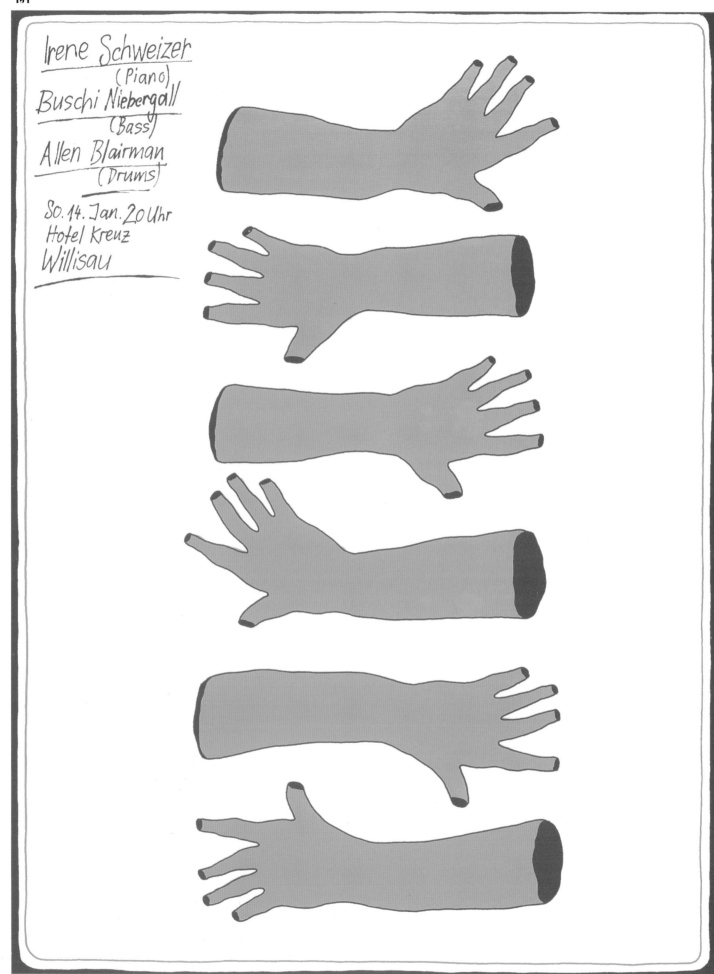

Irene Schweizer
(Piano)
Buschi Niebergall
(Bass)
Allen Blairman
(Drums)

So. 14. Jan. 20 Uhr
Hotel Kreuz
Willisau

2 "Irene Schweizer Trio" 「イレーネ・シュバイツァー・トリオ」1973

CECIL TAYLOR SOLO
WILLISAU FREITAG 29.OKT 20.30 UHR MOHREN

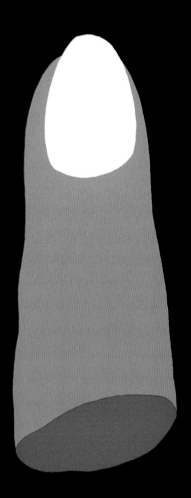

3 "Cecil Taylor Solo" 「セシル・テイラー・ソロ」 1989

4 "Daniel Humair Reunion" 「ダニエル・ユメール・リユニオン」 1988

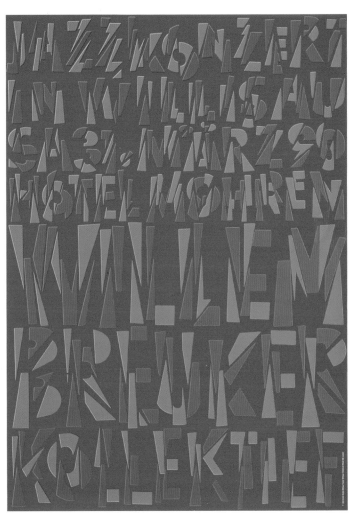

6 "Willem Breuker Kollektief" 「ウィレム・ブライカー・コレクティーフ」 1990

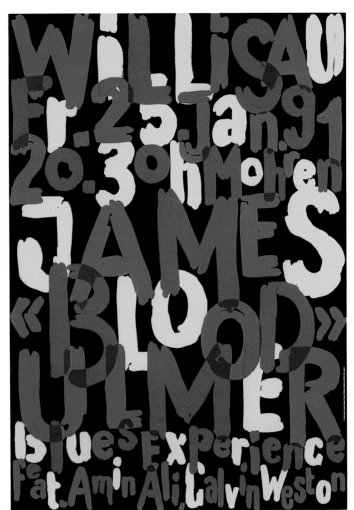

5 "James Blood Ulmer" 「ジェームズ・ブラッド・ウルマー」 1991

7 "Miniature" 「ミニアチュール」 1990

JAZZ FESTIVAL WILLISAU 89   31 AUG – 3 SEPT

8 "Jazz Festival Willisau" 「ヴィリザウジャズフェスティバル」 1989

9 "Tania Maria" 「タニア・マリア」 1988

10 "South African Jazz Night" 「南アフリカのジャズの夕べ」1990

11 "New New York Jazz" 「新しいニューヨークジャズ」1987

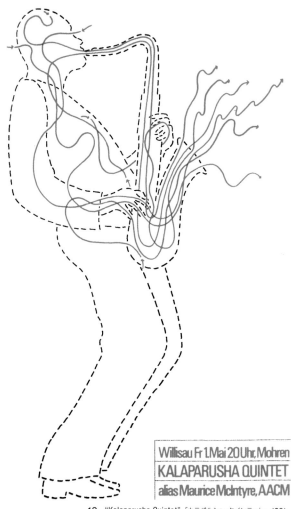

12 "Kalaparusha Quintet" 「カラパルシャ・クインテット」 1981

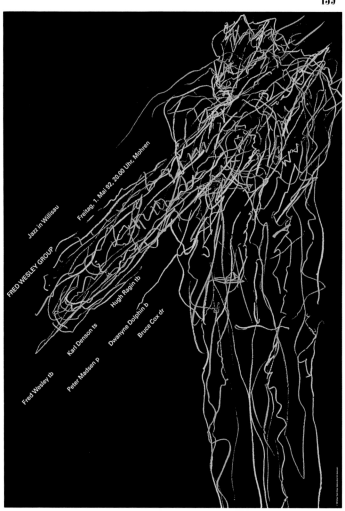

14 "Fred Wesley Quintet" 「フレッド・ウェスリー・クインテット」 1992

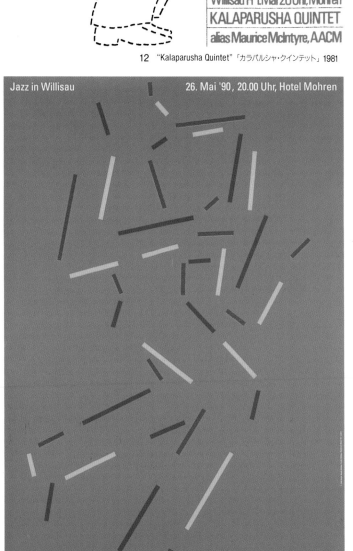

13 "Gary Thomas' Seventh Quadrant" 「ゲーリー・トーマス・セブンス・クワドラント」 1990

15 "David Murray Quartet" 「デヴィッド・マレイ・カルテット」 1983

Willisau Freitag 12. März 20 Uhr Hotel Mohren
JOHN SURMAN BARRE PHILLIPS STU MARTIN

Grafik - Studio Niklaus Troxler Willisau / Siebdruck Bösch Luzern

16 "The Trio" 「ザ・トリオ」1976

17 "Arthur Blythe Quartet"「アーサー・ブライス・カルテット」1982

18 "The Melody Four"「ザ・メロディ・フォー」1992

19 Recruitment poster for advertising firm 広告代理店の求人ポスター 1988

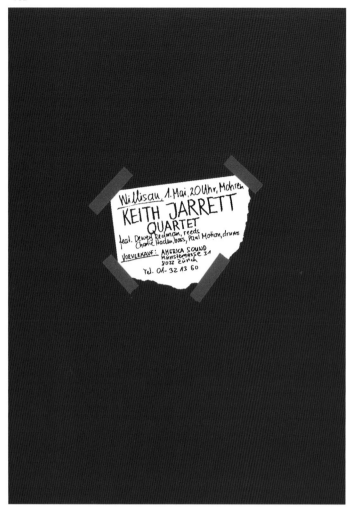

20 "Keith Jarrett Quartet" 「キース・ジャレット・カルテット」 1976

WILLISAU SO 6.MÄRZ 17 UHR MOHREN

MARIA JOAO VOCAL AKI TAKASE PIANO

22 "Maria Joao/Aki Takase" 「マリア・ジョアン／高瀬アキ」 1988

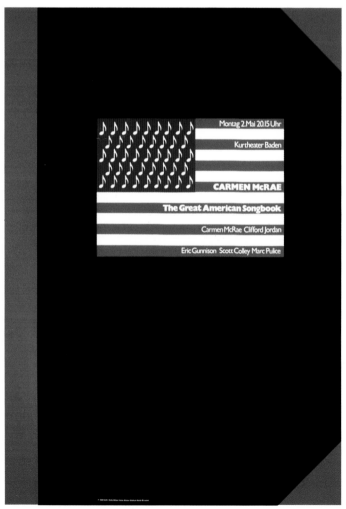

21 "Carmen McRae/The Great American Songbook" 「カーメン・マクレエ／グレート・アメリカン・ソングブック」 1988

Willisau, Freitag 18. Nov. 20.00 Uhr Hotel Mohren   DOPPEL KONZERT

MIKE OSBORNE QUINTET   IRENE SCHWEIZER TRIO

23 "Mike Osborne Quintet/Irene Schwezer Trio"「マイク・オズボーン・クインテット／イレーネ・シュバイツァー・トリオ」1977

EIKO ISHIOKA 石岡瑛子

Mark Holborn マーク・ホルボーン

Throughout her career Eiko Ishioka has always appeared to deny the categories of her work that commentators wish to ascribe to her. Her career can be followed through a series of denials. Since receiving an Academy Award for her costumes for Francis Ford Coppola's adaptation of *Dracula* in March this year, an accolade that many would regard as the pinnacle of a career, she has been busy denying that she is a "costume designer." After being nominated for a Tony Award for her designs for the play *M.Butterfly* on Broadway in 1988, she denied that she was a theater designer. She received a special award at the Cannes Film Festival in 1984 for the production design of Paul Schrader's film on Mishima; yet she exists as a creative figure outside the world of cinema or the world of theater.

She has already transcended the role of graphic designer and art director, having produced some of the most striking posters, book designs, album covers and television commercials of her time. She has mastered both the two-dimensional graphic medium and the three-dimensional theater media, yet she encompasses all media almost without distinction as she investigates the psychology of design rather than the surface of design.

Ishioka's first, almost revolutionary, denial was to challenge the clichéd preconceptions of Japan which she encountered in America. Japan was not simply a land of cherry blossoms, sumo wrestlers and Walkman. She gave an important lecture at the Japan Society in New York denying the stereotypes of Japan. Although she maintains a studio in Tokyo, Ishioka spends much time in New York, Los Angeles and London. Like her friend Issey Miyake, she is no longer simply a Japanese designer. She is both Japanese and outside Japan, just as she is outside theater or cinema or even the world of design itself.

When asked by Paul Schrader to design the sets for *Mishima*, Ishioka replied that she had never admired Mishima, a writer whose position and writing had fascinated many of us in the West. She felt detached from Mishima's polemical stance, which she regarded as anachronistic. Schrader was delighted by Ishioka's response since he was making a film about his view, that of an intelligent Western onlooker, of the controversial writer. Ishioka employed Japanese theatrical principles of *kakiwari* to create two-dimensional theatrical expression. The international collaboration with an American director resulted in a film with intensely Japanese design.

David Hwang's play, *M.Butterfly*, had directly attacked Western views of the Orient as a kind of operatic fantasy, yet Ishioka's designs displayed the most dramatic Oriental motifs. She used an Eastern visual language to assist in the play's subversion of Orientalism. Even in *Dracula* she found the cross-over between East and West. Her notes state, for example, that: "Some of the Victorian bustle dresses I saw during my research were made with Japanese obi fabric."

It would be simplistic to suppose that Ishioka is constantly caught in the exchange between East and West. Her sources, as in *Dracula*, could be anatomical like the muscle structure of the human body or the scales of a lizard. She is curious and absorbing relentlessly as she crosses the world. This position, that of the observer in motion, is not necessarily one of displacement or alienation, but rather of engagement.

石岡瑛子は常に、評論家が彼女の仕事をあてはめようとする領域を否定してきたように思える。彼女のキャリアをたどるとそれは否定の連続である。この3月にフランシス・コッポラ監督の映画「ドラキュラ」の衣装で、最高の栄誉といわれるアカデミー賞を受賞したが、それ以来「衣装デザイナー」であることを打ち消すのに必死だ。ブロードウェイのミュージカル「M.バタフライ」で1988年、トニー賞にノミネートされたときは、舞台デザイナーの肩書を拒んだ。1984年にはポール・シュレーダー監督の映画「ミシマ」でカンヌ映画祭特別賞も受賞した彼女だが、映画・演劇界とは一線を画したクリエイターである。

彼女はグラフィックデザイナー、アートディレクターとして、印象に残るポスターや本、レコードジャケット、テレビコマーシャルを生み出したが、すでにその枠を越えている。2次元の印刷メディアと3次元の舞台メディアのいずれもマスターし、デザインの表層よりむしろ心理面を追求して、あらゆるメディアをほとんど分け隔てなく扱う。

石岡の最初の革命的ともいえる否定は、アメリカで目にした日本に対する陳腐な先入観への挑戦であった。日本は桜や相撲、そしてウォークマンだけの国ではない。ニューヨークのジャパンソサエティで講演をした時、彼女は日本に関する固定観念を否定した。東京にスタジオを持ちながらも、石岡はニューヨークやロサンゼルス、ロンドンで過ごすことが多い。友人の三宅一生と同様、もはや単なる日本人デザイナーではない。演劇・映画界、そしてデザイン界とさえ距離を置くように、日本人でありながら、外の人でもあるのだ。

ポール・シュレーダーに「ミシマ」のセットを依頼されたとき、石岡は多くの欧米人をその生き方と文学作品とで魅了した三島由紀夫を尊敬したことがないと答えた。三島の批判的な態度が時代錯誤に映り、彼女は違和感を感じたという。シュレーダーはその反応を喜んだ。というのも、この賛否両論の激しい作家を、知性派欧米人の傍観者という視点で映画化したかったのである。石岡は2次元的な表現をするため、日本の演劇にみられる「書き割り」を用いた。アメリカ人監督との国際的な共同制作により、この映画は極めて日本的デザインの映画に仕上がった。

デビッド・ホワンの演劇「M.バタフライ」は、欧米人が抱くオペラ的空想のような東洋趣味に真っ向から挑戦する内容だったが、石岡のデザインには極めて劇的な東洋のモチーフが見られた。東洋趣味を打倒する演劇で、東洋の視覚言語を用いたのである。「ドラキュラ」の仕事でさえ、彼女は東西の交差を見出している。彼女の手記には次のように書かれている。「ビクトリア朝の腰当て付きドレスを研究すると、和服の帯地が使われたものがあった」

石岡がいつも東西の狭間で闘っていると考えるのは短絡的であろう。彼女がデザインの参考とする資料は、「ドラキュラ」でみられたように、人体の筋肉構造のような解剖学的なものだったり、爬虫類のうろこや革だったりする。好奇心が旺盛な彼女は、世界を飛び回っている間中、絶えず何かを吸収する。この動くオブザーバーという（常に一歩外に立ってクリエイトする）立場は、追放されたり疎遠になったりした結果ではなく、むしろあらゆるものに夢中になるためなのである。

1　Film poster　映画ポスター　1992

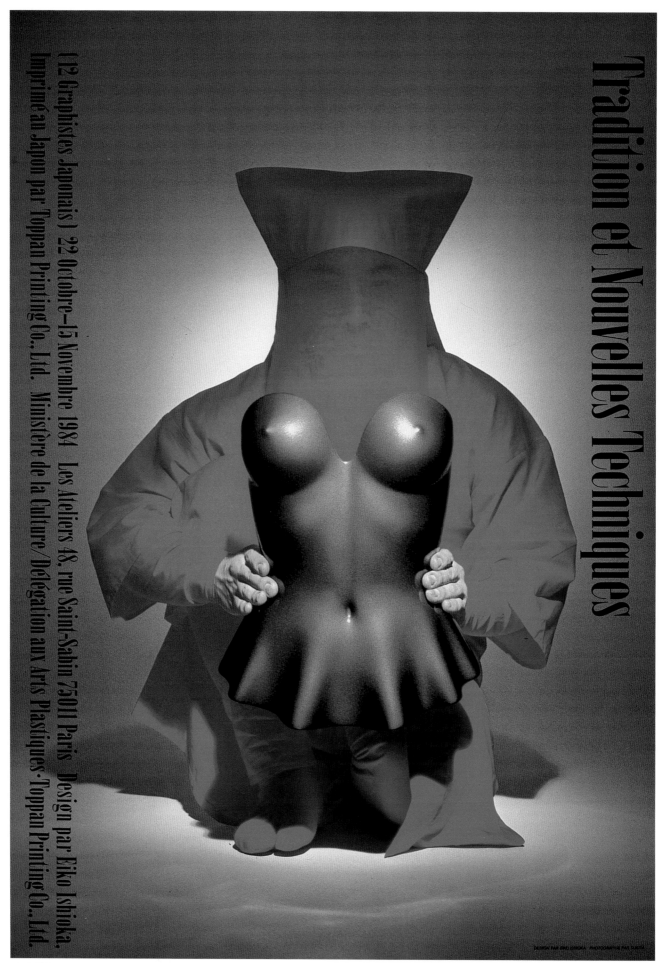

（12 Graphistes Japonais）22 Octobre—15 Novembre 1984 Les Ateliers 48, rue Saint-Sabin 75011 Paris Design par Eiko Ishioka, Imprimé au Japon par Toppan Printing Co., Ltd. Ministère de la Culture/Délégation aux Arts Plastiques·Toppan Printing Co., Ltd.

Tradition et Nouvelles Techniques

DESIGN PAR EIKO ISHIOKA PHOTOGRAPHIE PAR SUKITA

2 Exhibition poster 展覧会ポスター 1984 Photo: Masayoshi Sukita

イノセント

L'INNOCENTE
A FILM BY LUCHINO VISCONTI
ルキノ・ヴィスコンティ監督作品

愛は選ぶことができるか？
映画芸術最大の巨匠が生涯の力を傾けて
苦悩する世界に贈る哀切なる遺言

3　Film poster　映画ポスター　1978　Photo: Kazumi Kurigami

女は外の国を肌で知る

4　　4-5　Posters for fashion tenant building　ファッションビルのポスター　1975　Photos: Nariaki Yokosuka

6　Film poster　映画ポスター　1983　Illustration: Haruo Takino

7　Film poster　映画ポスター　1979　Illustration: Haruo Takino

旅にでる一冊
角川文庫

9

9-10 Posters for fashion tenant building ファッションビルのポスター 1980 Photos: Kazumi Kurigami

11 Poster for clothing manufacturer アパレルメーカーのポスター **1985** Photo: Denis Pier

12 Works anthology 作品集 1983 Photos: Kazumi Kurigami

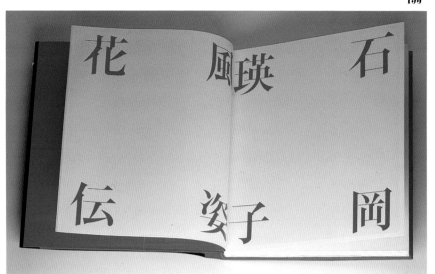

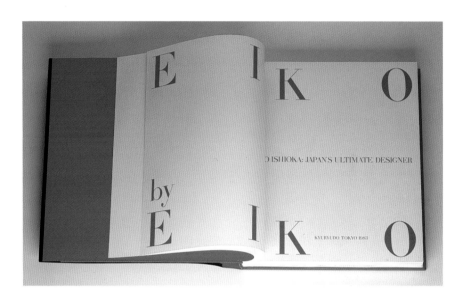

LENI
RIEFENSTAHL
LIFE

レニ・リーフェンシュタール写真展—アフリカの異星人ヌバ
昭和55年5月31日（土）—6月24日（火）木曜休館 主催＝西武美術館 入場料＝一般500円/学生300円 西武美術館

14

14-15 Exhibition posters 展覧会ポスター 1980 Photos: Leni Riefenstahl

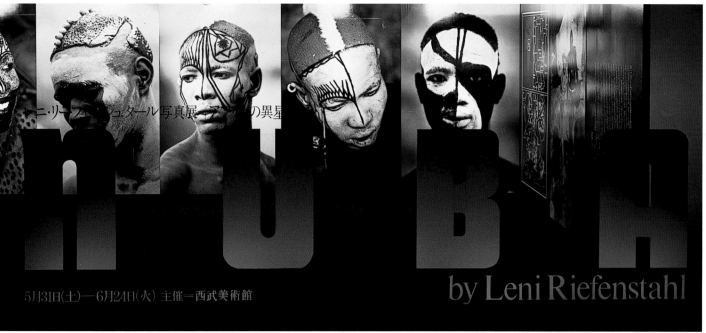

5月31日(土)—6月24日(火) 主催＝西武美術館

16 Window display for exhibition 展覧会ウインドーディスプレイ 1980

156

闇の中の愛を見たことがありますか。

17 Film poster 映画ポスター 1992 Illustration: Haruo Takino

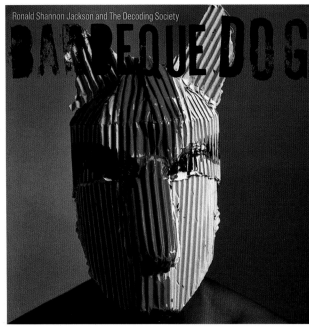

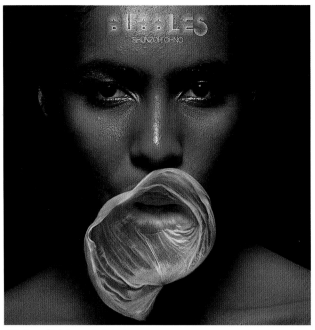

18 Record jacket レコードジャケット 1983 Photo: Kazumi Kurigami

19 Record jacket レコードジャケット 1976 Photo: Nariaki Yokosuka

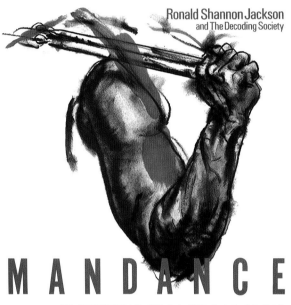

Ronald Shannon Jackson
and The Decoding Society

MANDANCE

20 Record jacket レコードジャケット 1982 Illustration: Katsu Yoshida

Masahiko Satoh

All-in　　All-out

21 Record jacket レコードジャケット 1979

ポスターを見るな。ポスターになれ。

PARCO

22 Exhibition poster 展覧会ポスター 1976 Photo: Koichi Inakoshi

158

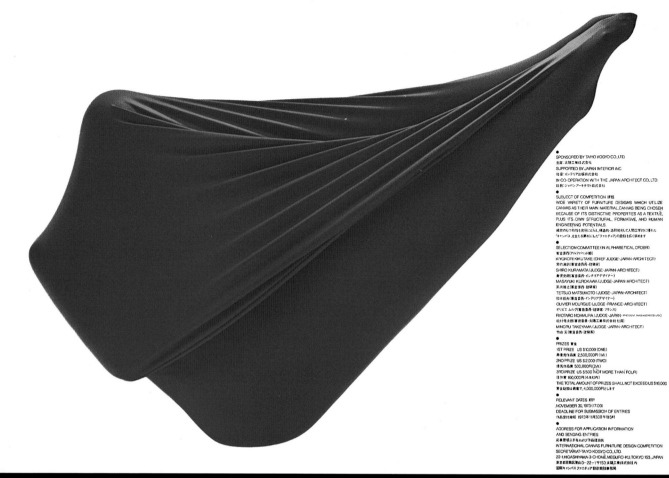

SPONSORED BY TAIYO KOGYO CO., LTD.
主催：太陽工業株式会社
SUPPORTED BY JAPAN INTERIOR INC.
後援：インテリア出版株式会社
IN CO-OPERATION WITH THE JAPAN ARCHITECT CO., LTD.
協賛：ジャパンアーキテクト株式会社

SUBJECT OF COMPETITION 課題
WIDE VARIETY OF FURNITURE DESIGNS WHICH UTILIZE
CANVAS AS THEIR MAIN MATERIAL, CANVAS BEING CHOSEN
BECAUSE OF ITS DISTINCTIVE PROPERTIES AS A TEXTILE,
PLUS ITS OWN STRUCTURAL, FORMATIVE, AND HUMAN
ENGINEERING POTENTIALS
成形のしやすさを充分にもち、構造的・造形的そして人間工学的に優れた
「キャンバス」を主たる素材にした「ファニチュア」の設計を広く求めます

SELECTION COMMITTEE (IN ALPHABETICAL ORDER)
審査委員（アルファベット順）
KIYONORI KIKUTAKE (CHIEF JUDGE·JAPAN·ARCHITECT)
菊竹清訓（審査委員長·建築家）
SHIRO KURAMATA (JUDGE·JAPAN·ARCHITECT)
倉俣史朗（審査委員·インテリアデザイナー）
MASAYUKI KUROKAWA (JUDGE·JAPAN·ARCHITECT)
黒川雅之（審査委員·建築家）
TETSUO MATSUMOTO (JUDGE·JAPAN·ARCHITECT)
松本哲夫（審査委員·インテリアデザイナー）
OLIVIER MOURGUE (JUDGE·FRANCE·ARCHITECT)
オリビエ·ムルグ（審査委員·建築家·フランス）
RYOTARO NOHMURA (JUDGE·JAPAN·PRESIDENT,TAIYO KOGYO CO.,LTD.)
能村龍太郎（審査委員長·太陽工業株式会社社長）
MINORU TAKEYAMA (JUDGE·JAPAN·ARCHITECT)
竹山実（審査委員·建築家）

PRIZES 賞金
1ST PRIZE US $10,000 (ONE)
最優秀作品賞 2,500,000円（1人）
2ND PRIZE US $2,000 (TWO)
優秀作品賞 500,000円（2人）
3RD PRIZE US $500 (NOT MORE THAN FOUR)
佳作賞 100,000円（4人以内）
THE TOTAL AMOUNT OF PRIZES SHALL NOT EXCEED US $18,000
賞金総額は最高で、4,000,000円とします

RELEVANT DATES 期日
NOVEMBER 30, 1973 (17:00)
DEADLINE FOR SUBMISSION OF ENTRIES
作品応募締切 1973年11月30日午後5時

ADDRESS FOR APPLICATION INFORMATION
AND SENDING ENTRIES
応募要項請求先および作品提出先
INTERNATIONAL CANVAS FURNITURE DESIGN COMPETITION
SECRETARIAT·TAIYO KOGYO CO., LTD.
22-1,HIGASHIYAMA-3-CHOME,MEGURO-KU,TOKYO 153,JAPAN
東京都目黒区東山3−22−1〒153 太陽工業株式会社 内
国際キャンバスファニチュア設計競技事務局

23 Poster for design competition デザインコンペのポスター 1973 Photo: Nariaki Yokosuka

NEW MUSIC MEDIA

24 Poster for music festival 音楽祭のポスター 1974 Illustration: Eiko Ishioka

25 Record jacket レコードジャケット 1976 Illustration: Shigenari Ohnishi

HOPE FOR TOMORROW / DON FRIEDMAN

26 Record jacket レコードジャケット 1975 Illustration: Eiko Ishioka

YESTERDAY'S THOUGHTS : ART FARMER

27 Record jacket レコードジャケット 1976 Illustration: Ryoko Ishioka

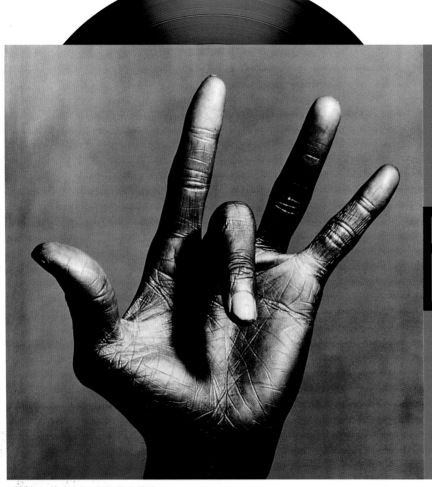

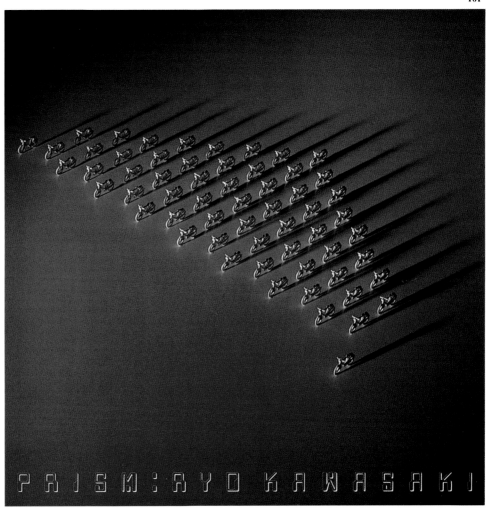

29 Record jacket レコードジャケット 1976 Photo: Katsumi Ohtani

30 Record jacket レコードジャケット 1976 Illustration: Eiko Ishioka

ある本である。
とても、パルコである。

THE BOOK.
VERY PARCO.

REPEAT. REPEAT MYSELF.

With my Guest.

31-34 Posters for fashion tenant building ファッションビルのポスター 1983 Illustration: Shinichi Toyama

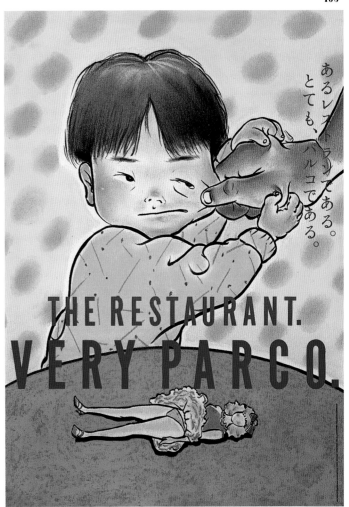

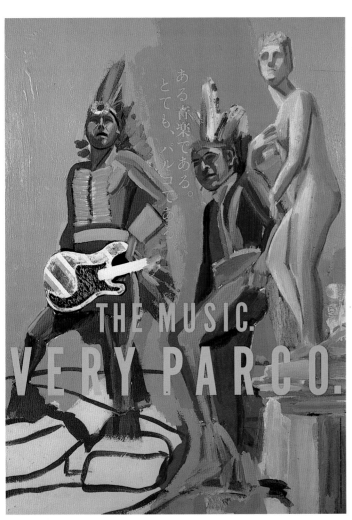

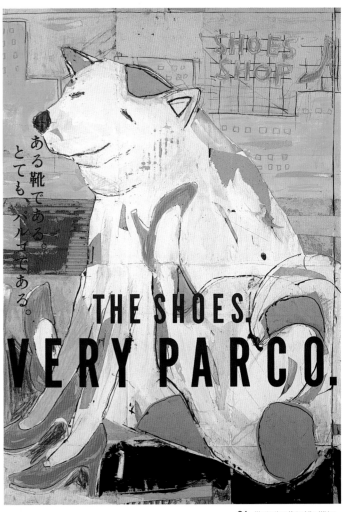

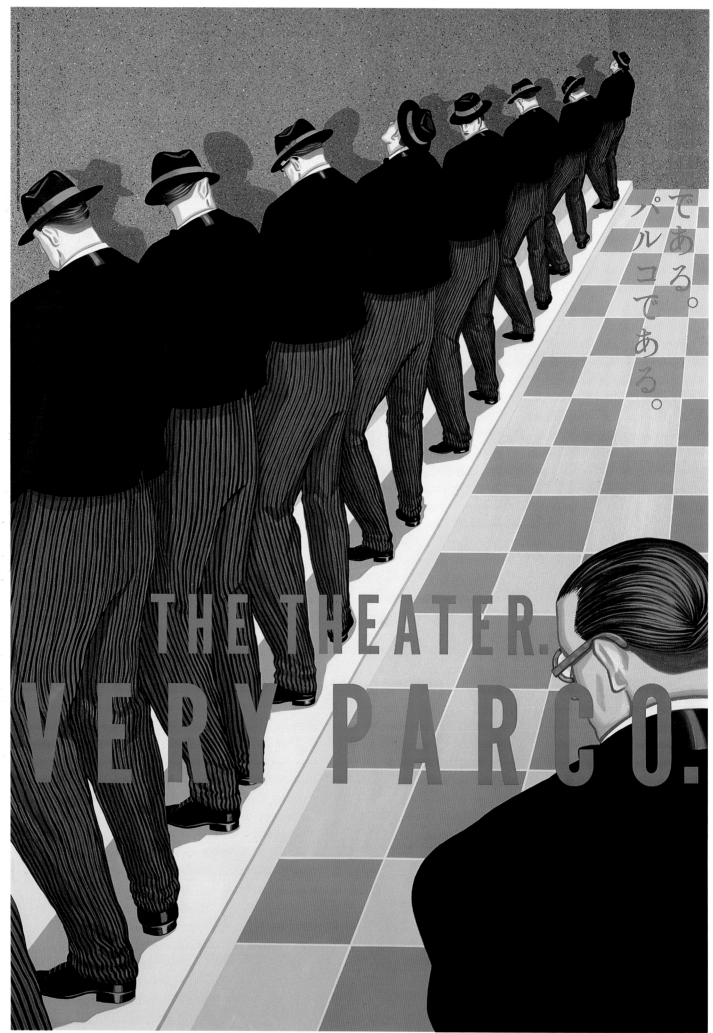

35 Poster for fashion tenant building ファッションビルのポスター 1983　Illustration: Kazuyuki Onda

1990 HIROSHIMA APPEALS

ARTISTS' PROFILES
作家略歴

FRANCISZEK STAROWIEYSKI
フランチシェク・スタロヴェイスキ

POLAND
1930 Born in Cracow.
1962 Honorable Mention at the 1st International Film Poster Exhibition in Karlove Vary.
1973 Award at the 12th Art Biennale in Sao Paulo.
1974 Award of the Association of French Film Producers at the 2nd International Film Poster Exhibition in Cannes. Silver Medal at the 5th International Poster Biennale in Warsaw.
1975 Award of the *Hollywood Reporter* of Los Angeles (also 1977).
1976 Award of the periodical *Projekt* at the 6th International Poster Biennale in Warsaw.
1978 Silver Medal at the 7th International Poster Biennale in Warsaw.
1979 Gold Plaque at the International Film Festival in Chicago.
1982 Silver Hugo award at the International Film Festival in Chicago.
1986 Jackson Pollock Award, New York.

Mr. Starowieyski studied at the Fine Arts Academies of Cracow and Warsaw. His professional career has spanned a broad diversity of fields, including painting, graphics, drawing, posters, and set designing for theater and television. He used the artistic pseudonym "Jan Byk" until 1973. He is also an avid art and craft collector.

ポーランド
1930 クラクフ生まれ
1962 第1回カルロビバリ国際映画ポスター展入選
1973 第12回サンパウロアートビエンナーレ入賞
1974 第2回カンヌ国際映画ポスター展フランス映画制作者協会賞、第5回ワルシャワ国際ポスタービエンナーレ銀賞
1975 ロサンゼルスの「ハリウッド・レポーター」紙賞(1977年も同様)
1976 第6回ワルシャワ国際ポスタービエンナーレ「プロジェクト」誌賞
1978 第7回ワルシャワ国際ポスタービエンナーレ銀賞
1979 シカゴ国際映画祭金賞
1982 シカゴ国際映画祭銀賞
1986 ジャクソン・ポロック賞(ニューヨーク)

―― スタロヴェイスキはクラクフとワルシャワの美術アカデミーで学んだ。彼の仕事は絵画、版画、ドローイング、ポスター、劇場やテレビのセットデザインなど様々な分野にわたっている。1973年まではヤン・バイクというペンネームで活動していた。また熱心な美術工芸品のコレクターでもある。

SAUL BASS
ソール・バス

U.S.A.
1920 Born in New York City.
1952-80 Freelance graphic designer, owner of Saul Bass & Assoc., Inc., Los Angeles.
1980- Partner in Bass/Yager & Assoc., Los Angeles.

Mr. Bass studied at the Art Students League in New York and Brooklyn College. As a graphic designer, he has made innumerable contributions through his well-known trademarks, CI, signage systems, package designs, symbols, etc. He also enjoys wide acclaim for his creative work for motion picture titles and as a cinematic director. Besides winning awards, honors and honorary degrees too numerous to enumerate, he is also a prolific speaker and writer. His works are included in the permanent collections of MOMA, Library of Congress, Smithsonian Institution, Cooper-Hewitt Museum, Prague Museum, Stedelijk Museum and Israel Museum, among others.

アメリカ
1920 ニューヨークに生まれる
1952-80 フリーのグラフィックデザイナーとしてソール・バス&アソシエーツを主宰
1980- バス/イエガー&アソシエーツを共同経営

―― ソール・バスはニューヨークのアート・スチューデンツ・リーグとブルックリン・カレッジで学んだ。グラフィックデザイナーとして、有名なトレードマーク、CI、サインシステム、パッケージデザイン、シンボルなど数えられないほどの作品を生んでいるが、また映画のタイトルデザインや監督といったクリエイティブな仕事でも広く知られている。おびただしい数の賞や名誉学位を獲得する一方、講演、執筆でも活躍する。その作品はニューヨーク近代美術館、米国会図書館、スミソニアン博物館、クーパー=ヒューイット美術館、プラハ美術館、ステデリック美術館、イスラエル美術館などの永久コレクションとなっている。

BORIS ZABOROV
ボリス・ザボロフ

U.S.S.R./FRANCE
1937   Born in Minsk.
1950-53   Studied at Minsk Fine Arts School.
1954-56   Studied at St. Petersburg Academy of Fine Arts.
1956-61   Studied at Sourikov Art Institute in Moscow.
1962   Became member of Soviet Society of Painters.
1981   Emigrated to Paris.

During the 1960s Mr. Zaborov received numerous awards in his native country for his illustrations for novels and picture books. After relocating to the West, in 1983 he won distinction by receiving the "Artist of the Year" award of Darmstadt, Germany. In recent years one-man showings of his works have been held in major cities in Europe, the United States and Japan.

ソ連／フランス
1937   旧ソ連ミンスクに生まれる
1950-53   ミンスク美術学校で学ぶ
1954-56   サンクトペテルブルグ美術アカデミーで学ぶ
1956-61   モスクワスリコフ美術学院で学び学位を取得
1962   ソビエト画家協会の会員となる
1981   家族と共にパリに亡命する

——— 1960年代は主に小説や絵本のイラストレーションで数多くの賞を受賞。1983年にパリで開催された個展がきっかけとなり、ドイツのダルムシュタート市の年間賞を受賞。同市立美術館をはじめ、欧米や日本などで個展を開催。

AKIRA SETO
瀬戸 照

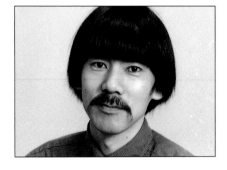

JAPAN
1951   Born in Kanagawa Prefecture.
1970   Graduated from Odawara Johoku Vocational High School, where he pursued a course in design.
1988   Became a member of the Tokyo Illustrators Society.

After completing his education, Mr. Seto worked in the advertising section of the Matsuya Department Store in Ginza from 1970 to 1971. Thereafter he began studying miniature painting under Tetsuomi Tateishi at Bigakko art school.

1951   神奈川生まれ
1970   神奈川県立小田原城北工業高校デザイン科卒業
1970-71   銀座松屋企画部宣伝課に勤務
1971   美学校細密画工房にて立石鐵臣に師事
1988-   東京イラストレーターズソサイエティ会員

HERB LUBALIN
ハーブ・ルバリン

U.S.A.
1918   Born in New York City.
1939   Graduated from Cooper Union.
1962   "Art Director of the Year," National Society of Art Directors (NSAD).
1963   Clio Award for Best TV Commercial at American Television Festival. U.S. Government Citation for design of airmail stamps.
1972   Cooper Union Professional Achievement Citation (and other distinctions in 1973 and 1980).
1979   One-man exhibition at Pompidou Center for the Arts, Paris.
1981   American Institute of Graphic Arts (AIGA) Medal.

In addition to the honors listed above, between 1952 and 1980 Mr. Lubalin received nine Gold Medals and eight Silver Medals from the Art Directors Club of New York; he also garnered over 500 awards from a plethora of professional organizations. He made significant contributions as a lecturer and educator also, right up until the time of his death in 1981. Today his works are included in the permanent collections of the Whitney Museum of American Art, Library of Congress, MOMA, Smithsonian Institution and the National Gallery in Washington, D.C.

アメリカ
1918   ニューヨークに生まれる
1939   クーパー・ユニオンを卒業
1962   全米アートディレクター協会より「アートディレクター・オブ・ザ・イヤー」に選ばれる
1963   アメリカテレビ祭においてテレビコマーシャルでクリオ賞受賞 米国政府より切手デザインで表彰される
1972   母校よりその際立った業績で表彰される(1973,80年も同様)
1979   ポンピドーセンター(パリ)で個展を開催
1981   AIGAより受賞

——— 上に挙げたほかに、ニューヨークADCより9の金賞と8の銀賞を始め、数々の団体より500を超える賞を受賞している。1981年にその生涯を閉じるまで、講師、教師としても貢献した。彼の作品は現在、ホイットニー美術館、米国会図書館、ニューヨーク近代美術館、スミソニアン博物館、ワシントンDCの国立ギャラリーの永久コレクションとなっている。

LOU DORFSMAN
ルウ・ドーフスマン

U.S.A.
1918   Born in New York City.
1939   Graduated from Cooper Union School of Art and Architecture.
1956   Citation for Outstanding Professional Achievement from Cooper Union (other distinctions in 1962 and 1980).
1978   Inducted in N.Y. ADC Hall of Fame. AIGA Gold Medal from American Institute of Graphic Arts.
1979   One-man show and 25-year retrospective at the Israel Museum in Jerusalem.

Through the years Mr. Dorfsman has received 13 Gold Medals and 23 Awards of Distinction from the New York ADC in categories as varied as print and television advertising, packaging, film titling, book design and direct mail. Other noted honors, among many others, are two Clio Awards for best TV and newspaper advertising. He joined CBS in 1946 as staff designer, marking the start of a four-decade relationship until his resignation as Sr. Vice President in 1988. Also active as an educator and writer, Mr. Dorfsman now operates his own design studio.

アメリカ
1918   ニューヨークに生まれる
1939   クーパー・ユニオンを卒業
1956   母校よりその際立った業績で表彰される(1962、80年も同様)
1978   ニューヨークADCホール・オブ・フェイム、AIGAより金賞を受賞
1979   イスラエル美術館(エルサレム)で25年間を回顧する個展開催

——— ドーフスマンはニューヨークADCより、新聞雑誌広告、テレビコマーシャル、パッケージ、映画タイトル、装丁、ダイレクトメールなど様々な分野で13の金賞と23の佳作を受賞。ほかにもテレビ・新聞広告で2つのクリオ賞を獲得するなど多数の受賞がある。1946年にCBSにデザイナーとして入社。CBSとのつながりは、1988年に副社長を退任するまで、40年にわたっている。教育者、執筆家としても活躍中であり、現在は自分のデザイン事務所を主宰している。

NIKLAUS TROXLER
ニクラウス・トロクスラー

SWITZERLAND
1947 Born in Willisau, Canton of Lucerne.
1967-71 Studied graphic design at Schule
für Gestaltung, Lucerne.
1971-72 Art director at Hollenstein Création, Paris.
1973 Went freelance.

During his career to date, Mr. Troxler has won numerous awards both in his native country and abroad. At home he has gleaned 14 awards in the Swiss Poster of the Year competition, and two Gold and 11 Silver Medals from the Swiss ADC. He has also been recognized internationally through awards from the New York ADC, New York Type Directors Club, at the Essen Poster Triennial and at the International Poster Biennale in Warsaw, among many other honors. He is especially active as an organizer of jazz concerts and festivals.

スイス
1947 ルツェルン州ヴィリザウ生まれ
1967-71 ルツェルン造形学校でグラフィックデザインを学ぶ
1971-72 パリのホレンシュタイン・クレアシオンでアートディレクターを務める
1973 ヴィリザウでグラフィックデザイナーとして独立
1966- ヴィリザウ・ジャズコンサートを企画運営
1975- ヴィリザウ・ジャズ・フェスティバルを企画運営

—— トロクスラーの作品はスイスの年間最優秀ポスター、スイスADCの金賞、銀賞など多数受賞しているほか、エッセンポスタートリエンナーレ金賞、ブルノビエンナーレ銀賞を獲得するなど国際的にも高く評価されている。

EIKO ISHIOKA
石岡瑛子

Photo: David Seidner

JAPAN
1983 Published an anthology of her works, *Eiko by Eiko*, in Japanese and English language editions.

1985 Award for Artistic Contribution at the Cannes Film Festival, for production design for the film *Mishima*, directed by Paul Schrader (1984).
1987 Grammy Award for Best Album Package Design, for Miles Davis's "TUTU."
1988 Nominated for Tony Awards for Best Scenic Design and Best Costume Design, for *M. Butterfly*.
1992 Academy Award for costumes designed for the film *Dracula*, directed by Francis Coppola. Selected as 1992 New York ADC Hall of Fame Laureate.

A native of Tokyo, Ms. Ishioka graduated from the Tokyo National University of Fine Arts and Music. After working in the advertising section of Shiseido Cosmetics, she established her own design studio in 1970. As a freelance graphic designer, art director, production designer and costume designer, she pursues her expressive endeavors throughout the world in fields as broad and diversified as films, theater, opera, video, exhibitions, advertising, publications, CI planning, package design and documentary projects. Her works are included in numerous renowned permanent collections, including MOMA in New York.

—— 東京生まれ。東京芸術大学美術学部卒業。資生堂宣伝部を経て、1970年石岡瑛子デザイン室主宰。以来フリーランスのグラフィックデザイナー、アートディレクター、プロダクションデザイナー、コスチュームデザイナー等として国際的に活躍。その領域は映画、舞台、ビデオ、展覧会、広告、出版、CI計画、パッケージ、ドキュメンタリー等多岐にわたる。1960年代、70年代は主として広告の世界で活躍し、東京ADC金賞および会員最高賞、毎日デザイン賞等を多数受賞。1980年代以降は世界を舞台に表現活動を続けている。米映画「ミシマ」でカンヌ国際映画祭芸術貢献賞を、マイルス・デイヴィスのレコードアルバム「TUTU」でグラミー賞を受賞。ブロードウェイプロダクション「M.バタフライ」でトニー賞2部門にノミネートされ、米映画「ドラキュラ」でアカデミー賞衣装デザイン賞を受賞したほか、1992年にはニューヨークADCホール・オブ・フェイム名誉殿堂栄誉殊勲者に選ばれている。

CONTRIBUTORS' PROFILES
評論執筆者紹介

JAN SAWKA
Polish-born artist and designer living in the United States.

HENRY WOLF
Art director. Member of AGI. Inductee in New York ADC Hall of Fame.

YUSUKE NAKAHARA
Art critic. Professor at Kyoto Seika University.

HIROSHI KOJITANI
Graphic designer. Director of ICOGRADA and Tokyo Designers Space.

STEVEN HELLER
Senior art director of *The New York Times*.

MARION MULLER
Copywriter, editor and art critic. Frequent collaborator in ad creation with Dorfsman and Lubalin, who was also her brother-in-law.

MARK HOLBORN
Editor, curator and writer. Special interests in photography and design, particularly works by Japanese.

CATHERINE BÜRER
Art specialist. Curator of posters at Museum für Gestaltung in Zurich.

YUSAKU KAMEKURA
Graphic designer. Member of AGI. President of JAGDA and Japan Design Committee. Editor of *CREATION*.

ヤン・サフカ
アーティスト、デザイナー
ポーランド出身で現在アメリカに在住

ヘンリー・ウルフ
アート・ディレクター
AGI会員、ニューヨークADCホールオブフェイム

中原佑介
美術評論家
京都精華大学教授

麹谷 宏
グラフィック・デザイナー
ICOGRADA理事、東京デザイナーズスペース理事

スティーブン・ヘラー
ニューヨークタイムズシニア・アート・ディレクター

マリオン・マラー
コピーライター、編集者、美術評論家
義理の兄弟ルバリン、長年の友人ドーフスマンとはフリーランサーとして広告を共同制作している

マーク・ホルボーン
編集者、キュレーター、ライター
写真やデザイン、特に日本人の作品に関心を持つ

カトリーヌ・ビューラー
美術史研究家
チューリッヒ造形美術館ポスター部部長

亀倉雄策
グラフィック・デザイナー
AGI会員、JAGDA会長、日本デザインコミッティー理事長、本誌編集長

掲載作品のご提供を感謝いたします

ヴィラノフポスター美術館
ギャラリー・アート・ポイント
株式会社田中一光デザイン室
大日本印刷株式会社